Prison Health

PRISON HEALTH

Travesty of Justice

SETH B. GOLDSMITH

PRODIST   New York   1975

PRODIST
a division of
Neale Watson Academic Publications, Inc.
156 Fifth Avenue, New York, N.Y. 10010

Library of Congress Cataloging in Publication Data

Goldsmith, Seth B
    Prison health.

    1.   Prisoners—Medical care—United States.
2.   Prisoners—Health and hygiene—United States.
I.   Title.
HV8833.G6   365'.66   75-15714
ISBN 0-88202-101-X

Designed and manufactured in U.S.A.

To
Sandra

Contents

vii

Preface

On a typical day in the United States more than 350,000 men and women are behind bars.

For society these people are in many senses "out of sight and out of mind." They are (for all practical purposes) denied basic rights such as the right of being considered innocent until proven guilty. For example, of the 160,000 people who are incarcerated in the 4,037 locally administered jails in the United States, 35 percent of the inmates have been arraigned and are awaiting trial, and 17 percent of the inmates have not yet been arraigned. So, innocent men and women crowd the jails of America—52 percent of the inmates in jail have not been convicted of the crimes that have put them behind bars.

Other rights denied these inmates are education, recreations, and medical care. Indeed, the 1970 National Jail Census reveals the startling fact that almost half of the jails in the United States do not have adequate medical facilities or staff.

This book focuses on health care in jails. It is neither a pleasant nor an encouraging book.

It is, however, a book that discloses the terrible conditions existing in one segment of the health care delivery system and that offers some possible solutions.

The book is divided into five sections: part I is a conceptualization of the problem; part II, an analysis of three actual case problems; part III presents sketches of a variety of prison people; part IV offers potential solutions and directions, and part V is made up of appendices that should prove valuable for those interested in prison health systems.

Seth B. Goldsmith

New York
June 1975

Part 1

Overview

CHAPTER 1

Prison Health Care—A Status Report

The Tucker Telephone not only shocked the penises of the allegedly uncooperative and incorrigible prison-farm inmates of the
Arkansas penal system, but it shocked the consciousness of the nation and awakened it to the atrocious conditions within its prisons.
As reported by the superintendent of the Tucker Prison Farm, the
convict doctor, a person with no medical or nursing training, was
responsible for most of the primary care at Tucker, sold medical
leaves of absence, ran an illegal drug program, and also functioned
as the primary "Tucker Telephone" operator:[1]

> The telephone . . . consisted of an electric generator taken
> from a crank type telephone and wired in sequence with dry cell
> batteries. An undressed inmate was strapped to the treatment table
> at Tucker Hospital while electrodes were attached to his big toes
> and penis. The crank was then turned, sending an electrical charge
> into his body. In "long distance calls" several charges were inflic-
> ted—of such a duration designed to stop just short of an inmate's
> fainting . . . sustained current not only caused an inmate to lose
> consciousness but resulted in irreparable damage to his testicles.

Describing the physical conditions of the medical department
at Tucker, Murton[2] noted algae growing on the floor, condemned
electrical wiring, poor sanitation, and unreliable flood protection
that often resulted in fecal matter floating around and through the
surgical and ward areas. Despite these defects and despite the
availability of an acceptable medical facility in an adjoining building (but used only for post mortem examinations following state-
ordered executions), the medical department was annually
licensed by the state "without benefit of an on-site inspection."[3]

National Studies

While what happened in Arkansas in the Prison Medical
Department in 1969 was extreme, the literature on prison medical
care clearly indicates that the organization and delivery of health
services within penal institutions is less than satisfactory and has
been so for quite some time.

For example, in 1929 the National Society of Penal Information supported a study, under the direction of Dr. Frank Rector, that looked into the status of personal and public health services in prisons.[4]

The objective of Rector's 13-month survey was the provision of information on prison health conditions "which might be of material assistance to prison authorities in the improvement of such conditions and possibly bring a standardization of health and hospital practices in penal institutions."[5] After more than 100 prison visits and consultations with specialists, Rector delineated standards of medical care that were attainable in 1929, that are attainable today, and that are yet unattained in a large part of the United States. The standards recommended included intake and pre-discharge or parole physical examinations for all inmates to be done by a "competent physician," including "a dental examination, distant and near tests for vision, blood tests for syphilis, urinalysis on all persons over forty years of age, and other laboratory tests as indicated."[6] Other standards[7] suggested by Rector and his group were (a) 1 physician per 500 inmates and an additional physician for each extra 1,000 inmates, (b) daily sick call to be held by a physician who would also dispense drugs, (c) complete dental care, and (d) complete optometric care.

What has happened since 1929? Most studies suggest that the prison health situation now is as bad as it was then. One research report, however, offers contrary findings.[8] In this study, Aker mailed 110 questionnaires to state correctional department administrators of large state penitentiaries for men (average size was more than 1,000 inmates). Despite a response rate of 74.5 percent, Aker was confident enough about the results to conclude that (a) the capabilities of prisons in meeting inmates' needs are greatly improved over those in 1929, (b) the supply of medical facilities in prisons exceeds that for the nation as a whole, (c) the ratio of physicians and hospital beds to the population is greater for prisons than for the nation, and (d) medical care available in state prisons was as adequate as that found in the community hospital.[9]

A more recent national study on prison health was a mid-1972 joint undertaking of the American Medical Association and the American Bar Association. Their four-page, self-administered questionnaire survey of more than 2,000 jails gathered information on available services, inmates' use of health services, staffing patterns, funding, physician reimbursement arrangements, operating procedures, and relationships with local medical societies. The survey revealed that there are general needs for more adequate funding, planning, and public support and specific needs for health services standards, improved facilities, more manpower, personnel to handle mentally disturbed inmates, drug control procedures, and facilities for severely disturbed psychiatric prisoners.[10]

Unfortunately, the value of the Rector, Aker, and American Medical Association studies is in large part mitigated because of significant and similar methodological limitations. Specifically, both the Aker and American Medical Association studies asked a sample of respondents to fill out questionnaires that were self-rating forms. With such a questionnaire, special precautions should be taken to insure that the data collected are reliable. No such indicators of reliability were apparent in either study.

The Rector study, certainly the most comprehensive of the three, also collected information by using a structured questionnaire but, "The same individual visited all the institutions and secured at first hand the data on which [the] report is based. By this method the influence of the human equation in the estimation of work being done has, it is believed, been reduced to the lowest point possible."[11]

Is a one-day visit a satisfactory indicator of the consistency and objectivity of data? Probably not. Numerous anthropological and managerial research projects have demonstrated that considerably more than one day of observation is necessary to realistically appraise the operations of an organization or a human being. Studies that fail to recognize this reality tend to legitimize data that are less than adequate; in the instance of prison health care, legitimized, but inadequate, data can be more dysfunctional than no data.

State and Local Studies

In the past few years a heightened concern about prison health care has resulted in numerous studies of medical care in county or state prisons. These studies are important because one can see emerging from them an obvious pattern of inadequate facilities and personnel and a probable need for medical services.

For example, a 1967 study of three prison hospitals in California indicated that although the beds were not conducive to rest, all the hospitals did give intake physical examinations, including X-rays, urine analysis, and psychological testing.[12] The primary recommendation of this study was similar to that of Rector's (some 40 years earlier), that is, an appropriate staffing ratio for the penal institutions would be one physician per 500 patients.

Another California study, by Stokes,[13] was focused on medical care at the San Diego County Jail. Based on a limited review of records, a health history and perception questionnaire, and 40 hours of observation, Stokes suggested that inmates were lacking medical care; for example, she noted that the average time spent by a physician with an inmate on sick call was about 40 seconds. Regarding inmates' health status, Stokes noted that based on the responses of approximately 100 inmates to a history questionnaire, inmates were indeed in poor health. Unfortunately, this information is of limited value because, as Stokes stated, "A correlation was not made between inmate perception of health status at admission and the 54 percent of inmates with mental health, drug and alcohol problems, plus the additional 29 percent of inmates with special health problems."[14] Her conclusion that "the 31 percent who said they were not in good health at the time of their arrest constitute a minimum of the present people who should be seen by health care staff upon admission to jail"[15] is probably reasonable from a crisis-planning perspective, but it does not provide the needed information on the health status of inmates.

Personal communications from Dr. Jules Frank, medical director of the San Diego County Jail, provide another picture of health care at that institution, a picture developed from the responses of 1,788 inmates to intake screening questionnaires. Atlhough 19 percent of the inmates thought they were in need of medical attention, 87 percent said that they were not presently sick. Commenting on the Stokes' study, Frank questioned its statistical significance and relevancy:

> Anyone in medicine who has conducted any clinic, triage in nature, must recognize the fact that it takes very little time to order a liquid diet, to provide a Band-Aid if necessary or treat any number of minor conditions and minor complaints which constitute the majority of complaints found at sick call. In addition, with respect to her report, the San Diego County Jail has an average of 72,000 bookings per year and I hardly think the questionnaires given to one hundred random inmates have any statistical value whatsoever, particularly when the credibility of

their answers was not further checked. This could have been done very simply by ascertaining if they had seen physicians outside the jail and simply calling those physicians and obtaining confirmation. It so happens that in the International Penal Digest, a journal written by ex-convicts, it was stated that out of 47 county jails in the United States, San Diego County Jail rated good, with the ratings being excellent, good, fair, bad or lousy. These ratings were done by prisoners themselves who were totally biased in this particular publication.

The state of Washington's 1972 study of jails[16] concluded that "sufficient medical and dental coverage is difficult to obtain in many jails. The problem is acute in some jails because of the doctor shortage in the community." A 1962 Massachusetts study revealed that medical care for sick inmates was adequate and that emergency dental care was available, but "in no institution are all prisoners examined."[17] Eleven years later, the proceedings of a conference in and primarily about Massachusetts demonstrated the continued existence of those previously identified problems, the seemingly ever-present difficulties of providing health care in prisons and perhaps most significantly, how slowly change comes about in prison health systems.[18]

Another addition to the literature, which demonstrates many of the problems of prison medical care, was the inquiry into Pennsylvania's prison health situation.[19] This investigation began with the traditional unproved assumption that "People confined in prison commonly enter in poor health."[20] The major recommendations stemming from this study are that the state should organize its medical care program for inmates, that standards for medical care be established, that appropriate facilities and staff be provided, and that the system be continuously monitored and evaluated.[21] The major contribution of this report is that it provides a good picture of the process of care in Pennsylvania's penal institutions. Unfortunately, little information or insight is provided on the health status of the inmates, the probable effect of intervention, and how one could best organize the system to provide comprehensive quality care. These critical questions are still unanswered.

A 1970 study performed by the Kearney consultant firm for the State of Nebraska Department of Public Institutions,[22] considered the medical service staffing at the Nebraska Penal Complex by evaluating penitentiary records and interviewing penal staff. Their study indicated that physician availability at the penitentiary (1968 average monthly inmate population was 725) and the reformatory (1968 average monthly inmate population was 228) consisted of sick call two hours a day, four days a week—a total of eight hours' medical coverage exclusive of emergency care. Additionally, one full-time dentist, one part-time X-ray technician, and one full-time medical technician (whose job was not defined in the study) were employed in the medical department. Based on their evaluation, the consultants recommended elimination of the medical technician's job and employment of a full-time physician. They noted in their report that "This medical coverage is less than what is suggested by the ACA [American Correctional Association] Manual, but it is sufficient for the needs of the Complex."[23]

What are the needs of the penal and correctional complex? Is a population of more than 1,000 inmates well served by one fulltime physician with no technical assistance? The arithmetic of the situation suggests that the Kearney evaluation is indeed reasonable, provided: (a) there is an efficient physician practicing full time (35 hours a week)—but in the Nebraska report half-time apparently meant eight hours per week of scheduled time and availability for emergency care, (b) there is a normal population of 1,000 inmates generating between 4,000 and 5,000 physician visits per year, and (c) that the 900 annually admitted inmates present the physician with uncomplicated intake histories and have few problems on the physical examination.

Clearly there are limits to the logic of this arithmetic. Does a prison population generate the normal number of patient visits? Who does the laboratory work? Who distributes and follows up on drugs? Who is responsible for medical records and medical administration? The Kearney recommendations do not adequately answer these critical questions, and therefore the general applicability of their staffing pattern must be approached with caution.

In another part of the country, New York, a riot in a prison located in a rural community, eventually resulted in death, destruction, and an investigation into the health program at Attica. In this study, it was noted that "medical care was one of the primary inmates' grievances."[24] Despite this finding, the report of the special commission noted that the "ratio of doctors to prisoners compares favorably with the norm in rural communities such as Attica."[25] The staff for this 2,200-man prison included two full-time physicians, who were at the prison mornings from Monday through Friday, and were on call for emergencies; four nurses; one pharmacist; one laboratory technician; and one secretary. The process of medical care at Attica was characterized by rapid screening by physicians, few diagnostic tests, and little sympathy. Interestingly, the consultant firm that performed the study offered the hypothesis that despite what passes for unsatisfactory treatment, the inmates are physically healthy and the problems treated at the prison tended to be fairly routine and minor.[26] The solution offered by the consultants was that "of some alternate system for the delivery of care in which [the] essential services are provided for the inmates of Attica by a larger well-staffed medical center or inmates in need of care are transferred to some facility with large enough volume to support more comprehensive staffing patterns."[27]

The consultants who reported on Attica also reviewed the prison health situation at the New York State Prison at Clinton and the Manhattan Men's House of Detention (the Tombs). The review of the 2,000-man Clinton Correctional Facility, which has a prison hospital, included two days of visiting, interviews, and a review and analysis of medical records. In their study, it was found that hospital usage at Clinton was three times greater than would be expected from a general population and "The number of hospital days per 1,000 inmates was nine times greater than would be expected in an average male population with a median age under 30 years."[28] Several explanations are offered for this unexpectedly high usage: pre-existing health of inmates, convenience of medical staff, and need to isolate certain cases. The basic conclusion of the study was that "The present delivery of health care services is minimal, not because of the lack of dedication of the existing personnel, but because of the shortage of qualified personnel, needed technological equipment, and some needed physical renovation."[29]

In the 1973 Tombs study performed by E. D. Rosenfeld Associates, it was noted that the medical component of this 1,000-man institution was somewhat inadequate, not only in terms of physical facilities but also in terms of delivering medical care.[30] For example, it was found that "insufficient physician time is being spent at the physical examination room and at the medical clinic to adequately examine, diagnose, and treat inmates" and that "sick call procedures do not permit adequate screening of inmates having medical complaints."[31] Indeed, the following statement from the Tombs report rings true not only for the Manhattan House of Detention but for countless other penal institutions:[32]

> The overall organization of health care services at the Tombs Prison is weak and fragmented. There is little evidence of effective and imaginative leadership; nor is there any sense of control or accountability. The various programs function in a disconnected manner and have not been drawn together into a coherent and continuous framework.

Before the Rosenfeld report, the Tombs and the other jails in New York City had been investigated by various groups and individuals—all with similar conclusions.[33] [34] One report of such an investigation, by Richard W. Nathan,[35] documented the medical care deprivation in New York City's correctional institutions and provided data on the massive expenditures required to operate the jails—more than $18 million was budgeted for fiscal year 1971. Nathan noted that:

> These resources currently provide approximately 7.9 physician hours per inmate per year. They permit sick call visits and initial admission inspections averaging two minutes apiece and specialty care when absolutely essential. . . . The mental competency examinations [provided in] inpatient psychiatric ward . . . cost per examination averages $1,770. . . .

Health Status of Inmates

With such massive expenditures as noted by Nathan, how sick are inmates? Some of the previously mentioned reports suggested that many inmates need medical attention, but how much?

In an attempt to quantify the health problems of inmates at the Tombs, Army reservists made three separate visits to the Tombs and performed physical examinations on three groups of inmates. The results of these examinations, which were reported in a memorandum of May 4, 1973 (Table 1), indicate that a large percentage of inmates are in need of medical attention. However, even these data must be questioned for a variety of reasons; for example, the inmates volunteered for the examination, and each

Table 1.   Percentages[a] of health conditions requiring medical care
among three groups of inmates, the Tombs Prison,
New York City, 1973

Conditions	Group A (N = 101)	Group B (N = 70)	Group C (N = 76)
None	72.2	70.0	71.0
Urinary tract infections	7.9	4.2	0
Chest diseases	4.9	4.2	0
Dermatological conditions	1.0	2.8	1.3
Eyeglasses needed	8.9	7.1	1.3
Ulcers and gastric disorders	1.9	4.2	2.6
Heart disease	2.9	1.4	0
Neurological conditions	0	1.4	0
Ear problems	0	2.8	7.8
Throat infections	0	1.4	0
Hypertension	0	0	9.2
Orthopedic conditions	0	0	3.9
Ophthalmologic conditions	0	0	1.3
Elbow infections	0	0	1.3

[a]Percentages do not total 100 because of rounding.

group was examined by different physicians and technicians. One
manifestation of these methodological limitations was the unex-
plainable inconsistency in the findings of hypertension in 9 percent of group C inmates but not in any of the inmates in groups A
and B. Numerous other inconsistencies as well as the
methodological weakness of this survey suggest that the validity
and reliability of these findings are limited.

Another study[36] included a review of the medical problems of
a predominantly white group of inmates in the Albany, New York,
county jail in 1962. This study of 500 inmates found that immediate
medical care, including hospitalization, was required for 113 or
22.6 percent, psychiatric hospitalization was required for 14 or 2.8
percent, and immediate medical care for a variety of conditions
was required for 68 or 13.6 percent. Other psychiatric evaluations
were required for gross personality disorders for another 8 or 1.6
percent of the population. Urine examinations were positive for
sugar in 31 inmates; followup tests revealed that 8 were true
diabetics and that 3 of these required hospitalization. Tuberculosis

testing revealed four previously unreported active cases. Eight inmates were found to have syphilis, and one had gonorrhea.

The Botterell enquiry report from Ontario, Canada, is one of the most comprehensive on a prison health system.[37] This investigation of jails, adult correctional and training centers, forestry camps, and training schools provides a detailed description of diseases and symptoms found among Canadian inmates in a sample of institutions. This information (Table 2), provided from intake examinations and sick call records, indicates that two conditions are common and prevalent in the sampled institutions—the common cold (acute nasopharyngitis) and drug dependence. Other conditions that contributed significantly to medical care in four of the jails were alcoholism, sleep disturbance, and nervousness, which also were prevalent conditions in five adult institutions. Other prevalent conditions in the adult centers were skin rashes and headaches. In the training schools, contusions, lacerations, and abdominal swelling were the third, fourth, and fifth most prevalent conditions. It should be noted that although all these diseases cause discomfort, few are disabling or lead to imminent death, and most are treatable within the context of primary care.

Finally, brief mention should be made of the author's report in 1972 of the Orleans Parish Prison, which revealed that neither the quantity or quality of medical care at the jail was adequate.[38] One aspect of the Orleans study was an epidemiologic screening of 50 inmates, and as previously reported:[39]

In a special study of 50 inmates in December 1971, no major medical problems were found on gross physical examination, although as can be seen in the following table, a large percentage of the 50 inmates complained of a variety of conditions. Basic laboratory workups, moreover, presented information suggesting that 14 percent might have had an active venereal disease and that 14 percent might have had a urinary tract infection. A review of the available medical records of these inmates showed that none had been seen previously for either of these infections. Perhaps of greater significance was the observation that 2 weeks after the abnormal results of tests had been returned to the prison hospital, none of the inmates to whom they pertained had received either followup laboratory work or treatment.

Table 2.   Health status of inmates in selected correctional institutions,
by percentages of selected conditions,
Ontario, Canada, 1972

Condition	4 jails (N = 700)	5 adult correctional and training centers (N = 640)	3 training schools (N = 237)
Alcoholism	9.8	4.0	0
Acute nasopharyngitis	7.8	10.2	11.3
Drug dependence	6.5	4.1	7.9
Disturbance of sleep	5.3	3.0	0
Nervousness and debility	5.3	3.4	0
Rash, skin eruption	2.8	5.4	3.7
Headache, pain in head	2.2	3.4	3.7
Abdominal swelling	0	3.4	4.1
Lacerations and open wounds	2.8	2.9	4.6
Contusions	2.5	3.9	6.6

SOURCE: reference 37.

Medical condition	Percentage
Frequent trouble sleeping	69
Dizziness or fainting spells	57
Nervous trouble of any sort	53
Depression or excessive worry	51
Pain or pressure in chest	45
Frequent or severe headaches	45
Venereal disease—syphillis, gonorrhea, and so forth	45
Leg cramps	41
Head injury	37
Severe tooth or gum trouble	37
Shortness of breath	35
Fractures	35
Eye trouble	31
Chronic or frequent colds	31
Palpitation or pounding heart	29
Recurrent back pain	29

Conclusion

Probably one of the best-known prisoners of the 1960's who has written about prison health conditions is James Hoffa. In a paper prepared for an American Public Health Association meeting,[40] he noted that prisons are "unbelievably bad for those who enter their gates either with incipient physical or mental health problems, or even for those who have no more than average resistance to physical or mental health problems, or even for those who have no more than average resistance to physical or mental stress."

Are his observations an overstatement? Certainly not! It is obvious from this review of the published literature as well as my personal experience as a consultant to many jails and prisons that a significant number of health facilities and programs are over-utilized, obsolete, unsafe—in a word, unsatisfactory. Indeed, they are simply a reflection of a prison system that appears to be in violation of the eighth amendment to the Constitution which forbids cruel and inhuman punishment.

Is the situation changing? Yes, but very slowly. For example, in New Orleans the new system is reportedly a considerable improvement over its forerunner. In New York, the quality of professional and nonprofessional staff and facilities is being upgraded and for a while the quality of medical care was evaluated by a group of health care professionals from outside the penal system.

These changes are encouraging, but much more remains to be done in this barren wasteland of medical care.

References

[1]Murton, T., and Hyams, J.: Accomplices to the crime. Grove Press, New York, 1969, p. 7.

[2]Murton, T.: Prison doctors. *In* Prisons, edited by G. Leinwand. Pocket Books, New York, 1972, pp. 200-201.

[3]*Ibid.*, p. 201.

[4]Rector, F.L.: Health and medical service in American prisons and reformatories. National Society of Penal Information, Inc., New York, 1929, pp. 1, 2.

[5]*Ibid.*

[6]*Ibid.*: p. 25.

[7] *Ibid.*: pp. 24–26.

[8] Aker, G. A.: A national survey of medical and health facilities in prisons. Master's thesis. University of Iowa, Iowa City, 1970.

[9] *Ibid.*: pp. 153–180.

[10] American Medical Association: Report on the 1972 AMA medical survey of U.S. Jail systems. Chicago, 1973.

[11] Rector: *op. cit.*, p. 3.

[12] Anzel, D. M.: Medical cre nthree prisons n California. Am J Corrections 29: 13–15 November-December 1967.

[13] Stokes, R. J.: Health care services in the San Diego County Jail. Master's thesis. University of California, San Diego, 1973.

[14] *Ibid.*: p. 93.

[15] *Ibid.*

[16] State of Washington: Jail inspection report—1972. Department of Social and Health Services, Olympia, p. 30.

[17] State of Massachusetts: The report of the Governor's Committee on County Jails and Houses of Correction. Boston, 1962, p. 12.

[18] Massachusetts Department of Public Health: Conference on Prison Health [abstracts], May 12, 1973, Boston. Commonhealth 2: 1–28, Fall 1973.

[19] Health Law Project, University of Pennsylvania: Health care and conditions in Pennsylvania's State prisons. Philadelphia, 1972.

[20] *Ibid.*: p. 1.

[21] *Ibid.*: pp. 10–13.

[22] Kearney, A. T. (consultants): Report to the State of Nebraska Department of Public Institutions on staff criteria for the penal and correctional complex. Lincoln, 1970.

[23] *Ibid.*: III-43.

[24] Attica: the official report of the New York State Special Commission on Attica. Bantam Books, New York, 1972, p. 63.

[25] *Ibid.*: p. 64.

[26] *Ibid.*: p. 68

[27] *Ibid.*: p. 69.

[28] Rosenfeld, E. D.. Associates: Clinton State Correctional Facility: evaluation and recommendations prepared for the New York State Department of Correctional Facilities. New York, 1972, p. 10.

[29] *Ibid.*: p. 35.

[30] Rosenfeld, E. D., Associates: An evaluation of medical and health care services at the Tombs Prison. New York, 1973.

[31] *Ibid.*: p. 30.

[32] *Ibid.*

[33] New York City Department of Health: Report of Task Force for Study of Department of Corrections Medical Programs. New York, 1965. Mimeographed.

[34] New York City Health Services Administration: Report on the provision of health care in New York City's correctional institutions. New York, 1970, revised edition, p. 3

[35] *Ibid.*

[36] Whalen, R. P., and Lyons, J.J.A.: Medical problems of 500 prisoners on admission to a county jail. Public Health Rep 77: 497–502, June 1962.

[37] Botterell, E. H.: Enquiry into the health care system in the Ministry of Correctional Services. Report to the Minister. Toronto, Canada, 1972.

[38] Goldsmith, S. B.: Jailhouse medicine—travesty of justice? Health Services Rep 87: 767–774, November 1972.

[39] *Ibid.*: p. 772.

[40] Hoffa, J. R.: The shame of our prisons: forgotten Americans—decaying health. Paper presented at 100th annual meeting of the American Public Health Association, Atlantic City, Nov.13, 1972, p. 1.

CHAPTER 2

Delivering the Care—Conceptual Problems

Consumers, professionals, and the organizational milieu within which prison medical departments find themselves provide the three basic constraints on the adequate delivery of health care in penal institutions. These constraints generate a host of problems, some of which are simple inherent in all health systems; others are unique to prison health systems. This chapter will first review some important general theoretical considerations and later focus on those special issues involved in prison situations.

General Theoretical Considerations

Medical care transactions are theoretically characterized by what Parsons has described as the sick or patient's role, and the physician's role.[1] Summarizing the sick role, one author notes its four dimensions:

> First, there is exemption from the performance of normal social obligations; and secondly, there is the exemption from responsibility for one's own state. These are the major privileges. The obligations have been described as the requirement that the sick person must be motivated to get well as soon as possible and to seek technically competent help.[2]

The physician's role, Parsons suggests, is characterized by the four values physicians adopt during the long and arduous years of medical school, internship, and residency. These values are: functional specificity, collective orientation, affective neutrality, and universalism. The first of these values, functional specificity, refers to the specialized role of the physician to provide medical care. One element of this value is that of technical competence. This suggests that physicians are, should be, and always should strive to be technically competent. Furthermore it suggests that only physicians have the technical expertise to handle the functions of medical care. Parsons maintains that physicians are expected both by themselves and by society to possess high technical competence and to devote themselves intensively to expertness in matters of health and disease.[3]

The second value is collective orientation. Here Parsons notes that "the ideology of the profession lays great emphasis on the obligation of the physician to put the welfare of the patients above his personal interests."[4] This value is confirmed by a study of midwestern physicians which demonstrates that physicians are, to a considerable degree, concerned about the welfare of the community.[5]

The third value, affective neutrality, demands that the physician act as a detached scientist, studying the situation objectively and finally making the logical, practical decision.

Affective neutrality is similar to the concept one author, Ford, labeled as pragmatism.[6] As an operational example of this concept, Ford found that doctors tend to have a positive attitude toward changes whose practical value they can see and over which they can maintain control.

Finally, Parsons points out that the physician's role is "inherently universalistic, in that generalized objective criteria determine whether one is or is not sick, how sick and with what kind of sickness; its focus is thus classificatory not relational."[7]

This theoretical model in large part explains why the unincarcerated person needing medical attention tends rapidly to lose control of his personal situation. Unlike the purchaser of a product or service, he is in no position to "comparison shop." Generally he knows little about what he needs, and often he knows less about what is happening to him and why.

Despite this lack of knowledge the patient is likely to answer the most intimate questions of a white-coated stranger; to strip naked and allow someone he may never have seen before to poke and probe the innermost recesses of his body; and finally, like a trained seal, dutifully to follow this stranger to a host of other strangers, who will systematically expose him to radiation, jab his body full of needles, and extract his vital fluids—all in the name of returning him to the illusory status of "good health."

Sometimes in the non-penal world the doctor or his agent in the health care system also serves a control function for sick role claimants. For example, in many industries a physician's certification is required before a worker is eligible to collect sick pay. Workmen's compensation benefits are another illustration of the power of a physician or a group of physicians which might significantly affect an individual's economic well being. On another level, clinical diagnosis of ill health can result in a person's being excused from familial or communal responsibilities, such as appearing as a witness in a court case, and it can also open the way to the benefits of rest and sympathy.

Specific Issues: Inmates and Staff

The routine problems of health care consumers are compounded when an individual is incarcerated twenty-four hours per day.

In the first instance, medical care in prison represents the fulfillment of the same needs that exist in the free world; that is, the solution to basic medical problems. A sharp chest pain, shortness of breath, a seizure, or the cleaning and bandaging of a wound suffered in a cellblock fight all require medical attention. The consumer in prison seeks care for these ills as he would on the outside.

However, to the inmate consumer, medical care has a number of additional dimensions: alleviation from boredom, an opportunity to build peer group status, a chance to get "currency," a possibility of escape from work, and, finally, the possibility of freedom. Each of these dimensions utilizes the medical system hard resources such as drugs, but, more important, each debilitates the soft resources—people.

The first dimension, alleviation from boredom, is probably, except for genuine medical problems, the predominant reason for seeking medical attention. Imagine being confined in a small cramped cell or day room area all day, every day—would not the idea of taking a short walk to another part of the institution be appealing? Would not the opportunity to talk to people other than inmates and correctional officers be worth the small cost of telling someone you are sick? After weeks on a dirty cellblock would not the thought of visiting with a nurse in the relatively clean atmosphere of the prison medical department be appealing? Clearly, the answers to all of these questions are *yes*; but such behavior, while perhaps a temporary respite from boredom for the inmate, is a serious problem for the medical staff which will be considered later.

A second dimension is status. Status among inmates in institutions is probably as important, perhaps more important, than status among people outside of institutions. Status comes in a variety of ways such as physical strength, criminal history, and degree of ability to manipulate the system. An individual who can demonstrate effectiveness in "conning" those in the system can build status—and probably one of the easiest marks for conning is the medical department. In some instances the ability to get through the screening process to see the doctor or nurse is a notable achievement which (when an inmate is not actually sick) is worthy of the accolade of high status. However, in other instances, it is akin to an initiation rite in that the accomplishment simply precludes the inmate from having a low status.

Economics is the third aspect of the problem; indeed, prisons have very definite economic systems that would in some instances be the envy of the gnomes of Zurich. For sale are such items as food, accomodations, peace and quiet, sex, and drugs. The methods of payment for these commodities are predominately cash, sex, and drugs. The medical department's involvement in this economy obviously resembles that of the World Bank. For example, if an inmate can convince the medical personnel that he is "nervous," a tranquilizer might be prescribed. Back on the cellblock, that pill may be worth anywhere from a few cents to a few dollars (in cash or services), depending on the mood of the cell and the general availability of the drug. At one jail, a freeze on dispensing tranquilizers resulted in the doubling of their cost within the jail. This results in a situation where inmates needing currency and having few other resources realize that, with a modicum of effort, they can visit the medical department and secure a no-interest non-returnable loan which, while not worth much to the medical department, is of substantive value on the cellblock.

The fourth facet, escape from work, is similar to any controlled environment such as the military; that is, there is a need for someone in authority to legitimate certain role behavior. A "rest slip" signed by the prison doctor is all that may be necessary for an inmate to be excused from the license plate stamping machine for a few days. The cost of such a chit may be minimal for the inmate, but the potential benefits are of such magnitude that the effort is worthwhile. Multiply that attitude by even a small percentage of inmates and the magnitude of the problem of those seeking to escape work via medical channels becomes obvious.

Finally, to the inmate the medical department offers another kind of escape—escape momentarily or perhaps permanently into the free world. Prison medical departments generally have limited capabilities and, because of this, often use local hospitals for medical back-up. A really sick inmate or an inmate who is a good con man must often be taken outside the prison to a hospital for treatment. This may mean many things in addition to good medical care: an opportunity to see friends and family in an atmosphere considerably more congenial than a jail, a chance to acquire new currency for subsequent jail trading, a change of scene, a chance to talk with new people who can perhaps assist in his release from incarceration, and, in some instances, a major opportunity for an escape. Few hospitals have prison wards and few inmates in hospitals are under constant guard—it only takes a few seconds to escape.

To the inmate then, medical care and medical departments serve a variety of important functions—unfortunately, most medical departments are unmotivated and do not recognize many of these "responsibilities."

The Professionals in the System

Physicians and nurses are in many ways the heart of the free world and of the prison health systems; because of this, both systems face many similar problems. Generally, the most obvious and pressing of these problems involve primary care: the difficulty of obtaining it, and the overutilization and abuse of facilities such as emergency rooms that are filling the gap in primary care. A brief review of how such problems arise helps in understanding the professional manpower problems found in prisons.

Earlier in this chapter it was noted that, during the young physician's socialization into the profession of medicine, technical expertise is adopted as a cornerstone value. This value suggests that technical expertise is important, and to those with the greatest expertise—for example, medical school professors—shall go the recognition and honors of the profession; conversely, lack of expertise relegates a practitioner to a position of low status.

The practical manifestations of this theory may be observed when one considers the problems of recruiting physicians to practice in rural America, in the urban ghetto, or simply as general practitioners. These alternatives are to a significant degree unat-

tractive because of the implied low technical expertise attached to
them. Practicing in rural America or the ghetto means being out of
the mainstream of medical care. Being a general practitioner means
not being a specialist—an expert.

An effect observable at the micro level is the problem
hospitals have had in staffing emergency rooms and screening
clinics. Physicians simply do not want to wast their time seeing patients with routine problems and complaints. Indeed, who can
blame them? Why should an individual trained in the fine points of
super-specialty medicine be interested in primary care?

After this brief discussion one must ask a fundamental question about jailhouse medicine: What is technically or intellectually
challenging about providing primary care to a small number of peo-
plè who appear to be basically healthy and happen to be behind
bars?

A typical day for a prison physician involves physicals, sick
call, and possibly an actual emergency. Physical examinations, as a
regular routine, tend to be unrewarding. Asking the same questions
and performing the same simple procedures is not very intellectually challenging. The military and even private medical groups
specializing in executive physicals have experienced considerable
difficulty in recruiting and retaining physicians to perform
physicals.

Sick call in prison is conceptually similar to the practice of
general medicine in the free world—with several major variations.
First, patients on the outside normally are not in a physician's office because they are seeking to alleviate their boredom, get drugs
for sale, or perhaps arrange a trip to another part of town. Clearly,
far too many prison inmates come to the medical department for
just these reasons. Second, patients in the free world have and exercise the option of self-medication, a privilege not available to inmates. In most penal institutions over-the-counter drugs must be
prescribed by the medical department and often by the physician—
not the nurse. Thus, conditions such as gastric upset, headache, or
perhaps hemorrhoids which are often treated by an individual with
over-the-counter drugs must become a medical department encounter. In addition, as noted earlier, because the prisoners are
not entitled to paid sick days the prison physician is put in the uncomfortable position of having to legitmate illness or injury so that
the inmate can be excused from his normal activities.

This responsibility also puts the physician in the uncomfortable arbitrator role; that is, he must adjudicate a conflict about the man's illness; on one side, the inmate claims that he is sick, and, on the other side, seemingly prosecuting the case, is the correctional staff. There is no winning situation for the medical department. A decision in favor of the inmate elicits no love, respect, or coorperation from the inmate (after all, he only received what he deserved), and in fact if the inmate has conned the medical staff the result is a massive influx of patients, all of whom seek similiar care "benefits." Correctional staff think that decisions favoring the inmates demonstrate both the soft-headedness of the medical department and a lack of faith in the correctional officers by health professionals. A more serious result of such a decision may be guerrilla warfare against the medical department by the correctional officers in the form of assigning the least useful and cooperative correctional officers to the medical department, or encouraging or discouraging inmates seeking medical care.

A negative arbitration decision results in the inmates' losing their confidence and trust in the medical staff with the possible undesirable result of the failure to seek care when care should be sought. Correctional officers are pleased with their powers and are encouraged to intervene in other, similar decisions and perhaps to make some medical screening decisions on their own.

Organizational Constraints

The final constraint on delivering health services behind bars is the basic organizational nature of most prisons and jails. In general, the primary goal of such organizations is custody. A jail or prison that fails to keep its wards incarcerated is simply not doing its primary job.

The second-order goal may be rehabilitation, which will include job training or behavior modification—all activities directed toward transforming people who appear to be social rejects into assuming what are considered socially productive roles.

To meet these goals most jails and prisons are organized into a pyramidal structure headed by a warden, sheriff, or superintendent with final authority for the day-to-day activities of the institution. One department which is responsible to the chief custodial officer will be medical: a staff department, which is generally entrusted with the health and well-being of the inmates. This particular structure forces the medical department to be accountable to the custodial structure and from this arrangement spring many of the myriad problems in jailhouse medicine, particularly the low priority given to health services.

Two factors account for this low priority; first, medical departments are not able to identify clearly with or contribute toward the prison's custodial or rehabilitative goals; second, there appears to be a lack of administrative leadership in many medical departments.

The first of these factors, contributing toward the custody or rehabilitation goals, puts the medical department into an uncomfortable defensive position because few of its activities are directly related to either of these ends. Specifically, medical staff are generally trained to prevent death, manage a chronic illness, alleviate discomfort, or cure an acute disease. All of these activities are related to returning a person to a state of apparent good health. While these may represent a reason for being for medical staff, they simply are not viewed as of the same importance by the custodians. In fact, to many correctional officers, medical department activities, which often require seemingly excessive movement of inmates, drugs, and vulnerable people (particularly nurses) on cellblocks, not only do not contribute to but are disruptive of basic prison goals.

Occasionally medical departments do make their peace—somewhat uncomfortably—with the rest of the prison. For example, some medical staff do become adjuncts of custodial personnel by using their talents to dispense tranquilizers in an effort to keep the prison quiet and to calm otherwise unruly inmates. What harm is done by liberal dispensing is unknown—but one must carefully weigh the problems of an active jail against the potential clinical and social problems of such drug usage. A different and perhaps more socially acceptable was that medical departments may become involved in a total program within a jail is through the use of plastic surgery and of psychiatry. These activities have strong proponents, who have demonstrated that in some instances recidivism can be cut down and inmates can be rehabilitated after a course of therapy or subsequent to an operation that corrects a physical disfigurement.

The second problem noted is lack of administrative leadership in prison medical departments. The two basic elements of effective leadership in such situations are an understanding of the total system within which the medical department operates and a full-time presence. Rarely are these two prerequisites met because the medical staff is frequently composed of individuals who have taken the job as a political appointment or on a part-time basis. Even in those instances when a physician or nurse is in residence full-time he or she is more often busy with clinical problems. In addition, perhaps because of lack of skill or interest in managerial activities such as budgeting or staffing, medical staff rarely become effective spokesmen for their departments.

In sum, one can anticipate significant problems in any health care delivery system that is forced to operate within a fairly constrained larger system. In the case of prisons and jails, medical departments are plagued by a range of special social problems generated by the patient population, further plagued by a host of professional staffing problems, some of which are related to general trends within the health system while others are strictly limited to correctional institutions, and, finally, medical departments are too often forces to operate with inadequate administrative leadership. The net result of these situations are the low status of medical departments and programs—all of which eventually work to the detriment of the inmates and eventually of society.

References

[1]Parsons, T.: The social system. Free Press, Glencoe, 1961, pp. 428–454.

[2]Bloom, S.: The doctor and his patient. Free Press, New York, 1963, P. 113.

[3]Parsons: *op. cit.*, p. 435.

[4]*Ibid.*

[5]Ford, A., et al.: The doctors' perspective—physicians view their practices. Case Western Reserve Press, Cleveland, 1967.

[6]*Ibid.*: pp. 144–145.

[7]Parsons: *op. cit.*, p. 438.

CHAPTER 3

Planning Prison Health Services

This chapter presents one approach to planning prison health systems; however, neither this nor any other method is sacrosanct. Moreover, meticulous adherence to a particular method is not a guarantee of a system's success, but a carefully considered and implemented plan is more likely to result in a system which is functional, operating, and capable of change.

The model presented here has six interrelated phases:

Phase I   Inventory
Phase II   Objectives
Phase III   Program Definition
Phase IV   Constraints
Phase V   Implementation
Phase VI   Evaluation and Feedback

Inventory

Phase I is that of taking inventory of the dimensions of the total prison health system and the medical department within the system. This entails the acquisition of basic information on the past, present, and projected abilities and capabilities of all medical department personnel; the past, present, and future budgets available for medical care; and the present services being provided by the medical department.

The gathering of data for Phase I may appear a simple enough task. For example, one might review the medical department's monthly or annual reports, and then check the personnel data. But, for one who takes planning and statistics seriously, caution must now be advised because data from prison health systems are too often found to be inaccurate. Like an accountant, the planner must cross-check each piece of information to see that all the necessary data have been reviewed, and that the available data tally properly. The evaluator must further check the data by independently observing the operation of daily sick call and by reviewing a large sample of the medical records. This fresh independent data could provide important reliability checks on the departmental reports.

Finally, obtaining budget information is likely to present some potentially difficult operational problems. One typical situation is that of identifying medical expenditures, which are often classified under non-medical departments or other hard-to-identify budget items.

Objectives

Phase II relates to the objectives of the medical department and the prison health system within which it operates. Objectives come in a variety of packages: actual, projected, and potential. All three are important to the planner.

The actual objectives of the operation are those that guide the day-to-day organization. In prisons these may range from elementary physical survival of the prison's employees to those of prisoner rehabilitation. In the most basic (and extremely prevalent) situation, medical department personnel appear most interested in providing the barest of services in the least threatening of environments; e.g., one finds physicians, nurses, and others dispensing care through ''bank teller cage'' arrangements. In such instances the professionals rarely come into physical contact with the inmates, and the entire medical transaction is often supervised by correctional officers.

Another extreme finds the medical department fully integrated into the total prison structure which is directed toward returning a useful citizen to society. A dramatic example (noted in another context in Chapter 2) occurs when a medical department is involved in a plastic surgery program that repairs disfigurements that might stigmatize an individual. A less dramatic program could involve optical or dental care for inmates. Clearly, none of these programs can exist in a prison in which the objectives are totally custodial and/or punitive.

The manifestation of the prison's objectives is most often seen in budget allocations, space designations, and personnel assignment. Money is the simplest way of demonstrating program support. An underfunded medical department cannot possibly provide respectable medical care. One must ask why it is underfunded. Is it because of a negative attitude at the top of the prison administration? Is it because of poor leadership by the chief of the prison medical department? Are the medical department's problems simply a reflection of the entire prison's problems?

Where is medical department located? Is its spaces adequate for its mission? If not, why? Are the medical personnel being supported? What changes do they want, and how have these changes been communicated to the decision makers?

A final example of the actual objectives of the prison is personnel assignments. Who is assigned to medical? Often, they are guards who are thought to be marginally functional. What does this suggest about organizational attitudes toward medical care? It suggests that the medical department is considered a low-priority area which does not require the skills and talent of efficient and effective correctional officers—a rather unhealthy situation.

What has been described, to this point, are the actual objectives—what the decision makers want for the future. While these projections may be of dubious reliability, they do provide a general road map for that future; they represent a verbal or written commitment that can often be used as a bargaining point for the installation of a program.

Information on future objectives can be obtained from interviews, memoranda, and personnel and fiscal budget requests. Public statements, particularly of political figures with high prestige, provide further information about objectives.

Finally, the planner should be aware of potential objectives, that is, objectives that have not yet manifested themselves in a particular system but may be the next wave of innovation. Recognition of such potential objectives allows both for longer range and more realistic planning.

A medical department must also be concerned about health status objectives for the total prison as well as for individual inmates. (For a full discussion of health measurement problems, see Appendix A.) The setting and measurement of such objective is a herculean task. What is an acceptable health level for inmates, and what is the responsibility of the prison vis-a-vis this level?

Program Definition

This should be an *idealized* phase limited only in a general sense by the obvious objectives of the total prison system and, to a much lesser extent, by the existing medical department. Programs can generally provide care on a spectrum ranging from emergency and primary care to tertiary care.

At the lowest end of the scale one would develop a program to minister to the most serious emergency problems. In such a rudimentary system, an on-call physician and an ambulance would probably be all that is required. A more elegant emergency system could include a variety of life support equipment ranging from a tourniquet to a defibrillator.

Midway on the scale might be a primary care system that does screening physicals, manages chronic diseases such as diabetes, and provides a range of first-contact care similar to the services provided in the office of a general practitioner. A few hours of physician care per day plus availability for emergencies would probably satisfy demand at this level.

At the far end of the scale would be a system that provides comprehensive care for a total population of inmates. Such a system provides a case-finding program, primary and specialty care, and in-patient diagnostic and curative services. Resembling the provision of all services to a small town, such a system requires a large number of full-time professionals and supporting staffs as well as expensive physical facilities.

The decision as to where on the scale a particular program should be is dictated by a variety of factors; one of these may be specific attitudes toward prisons and inmates. For example, a frequently heard objective is to avoid providing inmates with better care inside prison than they would normally receive on the "outside." Such an objective often precludes tertiary level comprehensive medical programs and, indeed, has a generally discouraging effect on all programs.

Constraints

Phase IV is constraint recognition and weighing. Manpower and financial resources must be identified and projections made for their availability. Limited resources preclude the implementation of the best-intentioned programs, while on the other hand the availability of resources may act as a catalyst, inspiring programs to move beyond their original goals. For example, what are realistic capital and operational budget projections for the prison and its health services? Is a fiscal or personnel budget of two or three times the present size even a remote possibility? Can a city, county, or state finance the construction of a new prison hospital or medical department?

The initial answers to these questions are most often "No"—"We do not have the money." But this "No" is often changed to "Yes" because of another, less quantitative constraint; that is, politics. In recent years, prison reform has become a significant political issue. Its political importance depends on a number of factors, such as the wide publicity the news media have given to the detestable conditions within prisons and the visibility of prison problems, e.g., Attica. These factors, as well as the seemingly pervasive issue of the 60s and 70s—"crime in the streets"—have made prison reform an important issue for all politicians. Furthermore, in many communities there are a variety of public offices directly concerned with the success (which is often defined as the quietude) of prison operations. Mayors or sheriffs may find themselves in political trouble after a jailhouse uprising. This trouble can then be turned to political advantage if a new and seemingly responsible program can be initiated.

On the other hand, the political climate can be of such a nature that the development or modification of a health system involving any financial commitment is virtually impossible. High taxes, increased crime, and perhaps a lack of serious trouble in penal institutions might act as factors to constrain health and other programs that are not specifically directed toward the custodial function.

People are the final constraint. One can dream of programs with greater ease than one can implement them. Assume, for a moment, that a great medical care plan requiring tertiary level care was funded for a state prison located in the center of a rural state 250 miles from a medium-sized city. Could one staff such a program? Probably not. The most likely result would be a beautiful facility that would be under- (if ever) utilized. Planners must recognize that individuals (both professionals and non-professionals) who are interested in prison health care are very few. Therefore, careful appraisal must be made of the human resources both presently and potentially available for such a program. A well-staffed, modest program may be politically, administratively, and medically more desirable than a poorly staffed "super" program.

Implementation

Phase V calls for action. During this phase the planner must make a synthesis of all the information and analyses of prior experiences with similar programs, resources, constraints, and projections for the future. In practical terms, it is likely that much will be unknown and that the planner will be forced to make educated guesses. Further complicating the planning process will be the availability of contradictory information. Nevertheless, the planner is being paid to produce a plan, and, in spite of the imperfect nature of the inputs, some plan or set of alternative plans must result.

The next step in this phase is analysis of the realistic costs of the different plans and the probable benefits accruing from the initiation of each of them. For example, if a program of complete physical examinations by physicians were to be initiated, the following cost/benefit situation is likely to develop:

EXAMPLE NO. 1

Program:

Physical Examination and Treatment Program by Physician

Actual Costs:

    a. Physician salary

    b. Equipment

    c. Supplies

    d. Inmate time (may be real cost if inmates are utilized and paid in penal institution

    e. Correctional officer time (transporting and guarding inmates)

    f. Laboratory technician time

    g. Laboratory time

Potential Costs:

    a. Additional medical expenses, caused by finding of previously unidentified subclinical diseases that now (having been identified) require treatment

    b. Lost inmate time (due to more medical care time)

    c. Correctional officer time (transportation and guarding of inmates receiving care for specialty problems)

    d. Space renovation for medical holding area

Benefits:

    a. Contagious disease threat minimized
    b. Physical problems that could cause patient and other inmates serious problems detected and corrected
    c. Staff not exposed to as many health dangers
    d. Improved health level of inmates
    e. Improved inmate morale
    f. Inmates physically rehabilitated and thus able to cope better in the free world, thereby increasing probability of reduced recidivism

Finally, recommendations for action must be made. These recommendations must consider the full range of problems facing a prison health service and, to be of value, they must be realistic. Why talk of a dermatologist in every prison when they simply are not available? Implementation flows more readily from recommendations that are sound and sensible.

Evaluation and Feedback

The last phase is that of evaluation and feedback. Any plan should be capable of being monitored, evaluated, and modified. If objectives for the plan are stated together with the measures of how these objectives are to be delineated and attained, then the evaluation problems are minimized. Confusion arises when, following Parkinson's Law, the program grows without direction or planning. Monitoring the program to see that it is accomplishing what was planned is one aspect of this phase, but evaluation is the key function.

Evaluation requires measuring how well the program is attaining its objectives, and furthermore, re-evaluating these objectives. Having made the evaluation, the planner must devise a mechanism that provides feedback to the program changes and modifies the program so that it can most effectively meet its goals.

In summary, planning prison health systems requires meticulous attention to the facts of the existing situation, clear recognition of constraints, and an active imagination that can visualize eventual order from the ubiquitous chaos.

Part 2

Case Studies

CHAPTER 4

New York City Prison Health—
A Bold Experiment

During the 1973 New York City mayoralty campaign, an acquaintance who was associated with one of the leading candidates approached me about prison health in the city.

"How would you rate prison health care in New York?" he asked.

"In a word—poor," I replied.

"But," he continued, "Time magazine said in a recent article that prison health care in New York City was about the best in the country and you say it's poor—how can that be?"

"Simple," I answered, "you don't realize how bad it is elsewhere!"

Indeed, in the early 1970s New York City aggressively tackled its problems of delivering health care to ten thousand inmates in eleven different institutions at an annual cost of ten million dollars. The basic decision to change New York City's prison health care system was made by the former Mayor, John Lindsay, and the then Health Services Administrator, Gordon Chase, but the implementation, operation, and, to a great extent, innovation in the system came from the Prison Health Services Director, Frank Schneiger. Included in these changes were twenty-four hour physician coverage, screening physicals, affiliation contracts with a major teaching hospital, increased personnel, and, finally, evaluation of the quality of medical care—the subject of this case study.

Background

A central concern in prison health services is that of improving the quality of medical care. One response to this concern in New York City was the establishment of an advisory group composed of outside consultants from the city's medical schools, hospitals, the New York City Health Department, the Fortune Society (an organization of former inmates), and senior prison health staff. This committee was to have the responsibility of continually evaluating the quality of medical care in the prisons, by biweekly on-site inspections of the eleven prison health facilities.

These site visits, which were usually two hours long, initially took the form of medical record reviews. A sample of approximately 30 medical records were selected at random and reviewed against a checklist which considered the presence and adequacy of the medical history, physical examination, treatment, and drug usage; in the case of mental health, long-term plans, diagnosis, general assessment, and referral were also considered. After these biweekly visits there would be followup visits by the members of the Quality of Medical Care Committee with the medical and nursing staff from the institution that had been visited the previous week, where a discussion of the site visitors' findings would take place. At these meetings, individuals from the institution would answer questions about the deficiencies of their program and attempt to work with the Quality of Medical Care Committee toward improving their local situation.

About eight months after its inception the committee entered a phase of self-review and evaluation. It was at that time that the following mandate was issued to the committee by the director of Prison Health Services:

MANDATE

QUALITY OF CARE COMMITTEE

The Prison Health Quality of Care Committee has as its primary functions the auditing of health care provided to prisoners in New York City and the advising of the staff and management of Prison Health Services relative to improvements in the quality of prison health care. Its mandate encompasses all facilities under the jurisdiction of the Department of Correction of the City of New York. Included are prisons, prison wards, and court pens.

The professional scope of the Committee's mandate includes medical services, mental health services, and dentistry. The Committee is empowered to review any aspect, professional or administrative, of the programs in these disciplines and to make recommendations for any of these programs.

Adoption of recommendations shall be by majority vote. Establishment of timetables for implementation of accepted recommendations shall be the responsibility of the Prison Health Services staff liaison. The Staff liaison shall report to the Director of Prison Health Services and the Chairman of the Quality of Care Committee or his designee.

Shortly after the mandate was received and reviewed, the committee made a routine site visit to the New York City Men's House of Detention, also known as the Tombs. This 1000-man facility, closed by Federal order in December 1974, was then considered to be one of the worst prisons and prison health departments in the country. At the time of the visit, health care was provided in several locations throughout the prison; for example, the mental health section had a special area which housed more than a hundred individuals on the eighth floor in crowded and unpleasant conditions. Other health care locations were the tenth floor (general medical and dental) and the first floor (admitting).

Organizationally, health services were delivered in several different phases. First, there were admitting examinations that were held in the Tombs receiving area on the first floor. Phase II involved primary care, which was delivered in a crowded and dirty area on the tenth floor. This space housed two physicians, several nurses, one psychologist, and one dentist. There was a small area adjacent to the tenth floor medical department where inmates were kept as inpatients if they were under observation for certain medical conditions that did not require hospitalization. Inmates in this area suffering from physical and psychiatric ailments shared the same quarters. Finally, some secondary and almost all tertiary specialty care was provided at Bellevue Hospital.

The underlying problem that generated this case study involved the admitting physical examinations at the Tombs which the committee found to be inadequate; that is, not a thorough examination but rather a cursory inspection procedure.

In discussing the reasons for these problems it was indicated that the Department of Corrections was partly at fault because of their continual pressure on the medical department to perform speedy examinations in order to avoid flow problems in the admissions area. Further criticism involved the examination space in the receiving room, which was noisy, tense, and crowded. The Quality of Medical Care Committee recommended staff changes such as increased utilization of physician associates, nurses, and clerks for clerical work and procedural changes which included the initiation of basic work-up procedures: for example, blood pressure examination and labortory testing of blood samples. Another idea advanced by the committee was the introduction of a 48-hour medical holding area.

At the next committee meeting after the Tombs visit, the major item on the agenda concerned the nature of the physical examination. What is an adequate physical? How long should it take? It was decided that an adequate physical involved a thorough history and the performing of a physical examination that acquired reliable baseline data on the individual. The consensus of the committee was that such an examination should take approximately fifteen minutes. However, it was thought that the admissions examinations being performed at the Tombs were taking somewhat less time. Both because of the sensitive situation between the Corrections Department and the Health Services Administration and because of the uncertainty surrounding medical activities at the Tombs, it was decided that the committee members themselves would investigate the Tombs Medical Admitting Area operation. This investigation had three dimensions; first, ascertaining the exact problem; second, developing a proposal for change; and third, seeing whether change was possible. If indeed change could not be effected, then the question was raised—What is the purpose of the Committee? Should it continue to function or should it go out of business?

The Tombs Admitting Area Study

Prior to the site visit at the Tombs admitting area a variety of documents were reviewed, including the following statement of policies and procedures which had been developed and were supposed to be used for all new admissions.

1. All inmates shall, when practicable, take a shower prior to entering the examining room.

2. All inmates shall, when practicable, enter the examining room clad in a towel only.

3. Medical personnel shall ask *all* of the questions on the medical history form, filling in or circling only the positive responses. NOTE: Questions pertaining to orientation, habitus, and suicidal potential shall be answered by physician.

4. The physician will then perform the physical examination. The examination shall consist of the following:
a) Inspection of the skin for needle marks, abscesses and venereal chancres. NOTE: Inmates shall be instructed to roll back their foreskin and show the glans penis.

b) Examination of the EYES: for icterus, injury cataract, glaucoma or loss: EARS: use otoscope only if necessary; NOSE and THROAT: for inflammation, abscessed teeth, growths.

c) The following:

    (1) lymph glands—cervical, epitrochlear, and inguinal

    (2) chest and heart—ascultation

    (3) alcoholism—hepato splenomegaly

    (4) any other examination deemed necessary by the examining physician.

    5. Serology—If no technician is available, blood shall be drawn by the examining physician, or a nurse trained to draw blood.

    6. The examination form shall be dated and timed to the minute and the physician's last name *printed* and *signed* in the space provided. NOTE: Physical exam forms constitute a legal record. Initials and illegible signatures are not acceptable.

    7. Any diagnosis and therapeutic programs shall be listed legibly.

    8. If lacerations or sutures are noted, a clinic date for the inmate shall be set for future care. This date shall be entered under "Therapeutic Plan" and the medical card shall be flagged.

    9. Abscesses to be viewed or treated by a clinic physician shall be noted on an "Injury Identification Body Chart."

    10. Attach a *flag* to the medical history form of any new admission requiring clinic treatment on the following day. All flagged forms must have the inmate's floor and cell location noted on the front of the medical history form.

How well were these policies being implemented? To answer this question, site visits were made on several different occasions and during these visits a number of physicians, psychiatrists, medical officers, inmates, and correctional officers were interviewed and procedures were observed.

It was found that a small amount of blockage occured as a result of the correctional process that required all inmates to have their property inventoried, and to be "stripped-searched" and showered prior to being sent for the physical. These correctional requirements were largely in concert with the pre-physical requirements delineated by medical.

Clearly, though, there was an element of hurry-up-and-wait philosophy operating, all in the name of security. Often there were as many as ten correctional officers in the receiving area and at

various times almost half of these were simply doing nothing—
merely sitting and talking with one another—essentially, being
available in case of emergency. Emergencies indeed did occur—
but with great rarity. One then must wonder why there were no
plans for using correctional officers during the large percentage of
slack time that was seemingly available. Inquiry into this situation
elicited the comment: "You are seeing it on quiet nights—we're
always having emergencies."

However, regardless of the staging problems, there was little
to prevent all of the physicians from taking blood and blood pres-
sures, or from examining the patients in a reasonably thorough
manner—aside from abdominal examinations, which were
somewhat difficult to perform for lack of an examining table.
However, when abdominal examinations were absolutely
necessary, the patient would either lie down on the floor or on a
bench outside the admitting room.

A large part of the physician's time during the examination
was utilized in the taking of a standard history from every inmate.
Some physicians had totally memorized the form and were able to
ask all questions by rote in less than one minute. This particular
function might well be carried out by a paramedic or someone with
considerably less training than a physician.

Space in the receiving room was indeed limited. However, a
large part of the space was wasted by two tables utilized as resting
places for clerks who, during the usual three-hour admitting
period, put in approximately a half hour's work on the methadone
program. The physical examination normally consisted of visual inspection of the individual, inspection of the penis, and in the case
of some (but not all) use of a stethoscope to listen to his heart and
lungs. Blood was drawn not as a matter of routine but when the individual physician felt that he had time to do so. Clearly, there was
no issue as to whether he did or did not have the time; time was in
fact available to draw the blood, but it was a question of the physician's own concept of work pressure. An additional task of the
physician was to mix methadone for the patients and to provide
them with general information about the methadone program.
Finally, since physicians on duty worked eight-hour shifts they
were also available for the rare emergencies in the court areas or on
the cellblocks.

Who are these admitting-room physicians? Basically, they are
young, well-trained, and bright individuals who are working in the

jail for the money, and not, according to them, because of their social commitment. All who were interviewed planned to go into private practice within the next year or two, and all felt that working in the prison was depressing and discouraging.

As a group they felt that when they started work in the prison they had attempted to provide admitting physicals of good quality. However, they now recognized that the work they were doing was less than adequate but they felt that this result had not been caused by their own lack of interest in providing quality physicals but rather by the fact that they had been beaten down by the system. The "beating down" process, they pointed out, involved correctional officers who were noncooperative, inmates who were always conniving and threatening, and a lack of assistance from the administration of the prison health services.

Interviews with inmates during these visits also provided some important information. For example, it was found that over 50 percent of the inmates had been incarcerated at the Tombs within the previous twelve months, 25 percent had been in jail in New York City within the last five years, and less than 25 percent claimed that this was their first time in jail. The significance of this finding is that physical examinations are performed on individuals who have probably had a physical examination the previous year but data concerning these individuals is simply not available. One can hypothesize from this information that it is possible to eliminate a large number of examinations, and, in the case of individuals who are having chronic medical problems, to develop a medical plan for them based on good historical data.

Quality of Care Committee—Conflict

As a result of these site visits the Quality of Medical Care Committee decided that some definitive action was required both on the Tombs situation and on its own role. Conflict began when a memorandum precipitated by the Tombs situation was sent to Mr. Schneiger. The memorandum was as follows:

> June 29, 1973
> The report of the site visitors from the Quality of Care Committee and the response from medical staff working at the Manhattan House of Detention indicates the fact that for a variety of reasons an adequate medical screening examination is not being performed on inmates entering the facility. Samples of charts re-

viewed continue to reveal the absence of vital signs being recorded on the charts—blood pressure, pulse, respiration, temperature, etc. From staff working in the reception area we have heard the fact that very little more than visual inspection type of examination is being performed. At the same time, the form which should be responsive to an actual screening examination is being completed, thus giving the false impression of a completed medical screening examination. As a case in point, without an examination table in the screening area it is impossible for the physicians working there to perform an adequate screening examination on the abdomen. Yet these are being checked as having been completed.

It is impossible for the Quality of Health Care Committee to accept and sanction activities which make a mockery of minimum standards of quality health care which we are all aspiring to achieve.

The Committee recommended early in its deliberations that a minimum time of fifteen (15) minutes should be allotted for the physician to perform his medical screening examination. The staff report the fact that pressure from the Department of Correction Staff prohibits screening examinations beyond five (5) minutes. As a result, much of the examination required to achieve the base minimum health assessment is being ignored and in some instances falsely documented as having been performed.

The Quality of Health Care Committee cannot accept continuation of such action. It is therefore recommending that if all efforts at correcting this situation fail, the Committee recommends that medical staff be withdrawn from the reception area and all areas in prisons where conditions are not conducive to health professionals practicing acceptable and adequate health and medical care services.

To have conditions continue as they now operate will force this Committee to resign since its existence will be meaningless.

The line had been drawn. A meeting of the committee was convened. The discussion was directed to the question of whether or not the committee was in fact a consultative group to monitor and evaluate the quality of care or an activist group to take public stands and serve as an active catalyst for changing the health care system for prison inmates. The major argument supporting the activist position was that the problems at the Tombs and the other city prison health facilities were so obvious as to make superfluous the function of the Quality of Medical Care Committee and that what was needed was not identification of problems but rather change.

The minutes of that July 24, 1973, meeting recount the "various strategies for improving the committee's effectiveness."

The following resolutions were approved:

1. Dr.——will write to several agencies (Board of Health, Fortune Society, Board of Corrections, Comprehensive Health Planning Agency, the Mayor's Office, the Department of Sanitation, the New York Civil Liberties Union) to explore the possibility of recognition and sponsorship of the Committee by those organizations. This was viewed as a way of increasing the Committee's autonomy, mandate, and thus its clout.

2. The usefulness and feasibility of further class action suits (such as the Rhem case) will be explored.

3. Methods of getting the Committee more political power would be investigated. One approach would be the first resolution. Other ways might include adding a publicity and media function.

Other suggestions discussed but not resolved were:

1. To provide blanket entrance rights to Committee members.

2. To document instances of both cooperation and resistance from Corrections.

3. To strengthen the Public Health/sanitary review of the city prisons.

4. To investigate the practicality (with the N.Y. Civil Liberties Union) of obtaining legislation to establish the Committee's independence from both H.S.A. and Corrections.

Arguments supporting a greater staff function for the committee centered around the perceived need to document the quality of care and provide hard evidence that could be provided to the existing and generally receptive prison health services administration.

The reaction to these events came as a memo from the Director of the Prison Health Services to the Chairman of the Quality of Care Committee on August 22, 1973:

I believe that a major effort should be undertaken to re-focus the Committee's efforts. The reactivation of the Committee at summer's end would appear to be the best time to begin. Needless to say, I believe that the Committee has lost its focus and, as a consequence, has had reduced impact in recent months. In addition, I feel that the Committee's credibility with both H.S.A. and Department of Correction staff has been eroded.

My feeling from the time of the Committee's inception, and one which I still have, is that this type of group can have a significant impact upon the quality of health care in the city's prisons. That impact will come with well organized, concise audit procedures, specific recommendations, and thorough staff follow through. I believe that my assignment of Mr.——as staff liaison represents a substantial commitment to provide the needed staff follow through and that it is up to the Committee to provide the audits, recommendations, and other services.

I do not believe that the Committee will achieve any success by constantly expressing outrage. It should be clear by now that all of us are outraged by many of the conditions in the city's prisons, but, in the final analysis, anger is pretty light work and does little to change the situation. Nor do I feel that gratuitous and ill-informed references to "standard H.S.A. variety" physical examinations serve any purpose, save further alienation of staff.

We have enormous problems, many of which are unlikely to be solved anytime soon. But I do feel that we have made a commitment to improving health care for city prisoners and that the Quality of Care Committee can play a central role in bringing about needed change. To do so, it must show enough internal discipline and long term commitment to withstand the day to day frustrations which are inevitable. I hope that the Committee's reactivation will mark the opening of a period of fruitful activity.

Discussion

The committee was not disbanded; the members decided that it would institutionalize itself within the framework of the existing prison health system to observe, comment, and evaluate. It would not seek to implement solutions; however, it would recommend change and it would monitor the implementation of those recommendations.

Therefore, the operation of the committee was drastically overhauled so that, instead of making visits on a weekly basis to institutions, its schedule would be modified to permit a variety of visiting patterns such as multiple visits to the same institution over a long period of time.

A second modification was the establishment of a shortened feedback mechanism: committee members and institutional staff met immediately after the site visit rather than a week later.

The third important modification was division of the committee into a number of separate groups each of which would have the responsibility for monitoring quality in different areas. Group A was to monitor medical quality through medical record review; Group B was to monitor nursing quality through inspection and evaluation of nursing plans; Group C, to monitor certain ancillary areas such as drug utilization; Group D, to monitor mental health programs, and Group E was to monitor management and administration of the health system. Additional plans were devised to develop for the institution a management review program which would include a self-evaluation package.

Other ideas such as setting up a separate budget and gaining official recognition for the committee were abandoned—the committee was to continue as a group of ad hoc per diem consultants brought together for the purpose of reviewing the quality of care: an idea that was seemingly institutionalized within the City of New York's prison health system.

During the next several months, key members of the committee resigned, ostensibly because of the pressure of other activities. One can speculate that their leaving may have been related to the sense of powerlessness that pervaded the committee or perhaps the frustration of discovering that the simplest change is often difficult to implement in a large, bureacratic—albeit captive—system.

In the fall of 1973 the Director of Prison Health Services resigned, and to many the last hope for an effective committee vanished with his leaving.

Within a few months the committee ceased to exist—its mission unfulfilled.

CHAPTER 5

Audy Home—Juvenile Justice

Little is known about the almost 3,000 institutions that serve as holding facilities for juveniles prior to and after court arraignment or while awaiting further legal action. One such facility is the Arthur J. Audy Home in Chicago, which in 1971 admitted 8,211 juveniles (approximately 70 percent male and 30 percent female) and provided 107,285 days of care with an average daily census of 294 and an average length of stay of twenty-four days.

This chapter is based on a 1972 study undertaken at the request of the Arthur J. Audy Home for the purpose of evaluating certain aspects of its medical department's functioning and to plan for the new medical department that was to become operational with the opening of the new Audy Home facility early in 1973. It should be noted at the outset that medical in the context of this facility excludes psychological and psychiatric services.

Methods used in this study included interviews with Audy Home medical department staff and the new Audy Home architects (C.F. Murphy Associates), a review of medical department and Audy Home official reports, and a review of medical records.

Limitations of this report included short and missing interviews (e.g., the Home's Director was not available), and time precluded both the examination of more than a sample of the medical records and long-term systematic observation of the medical department's functioning.

The most significant limitation was that construction of the new medical department was so far advanced that only minor changes could be suggested by the study.

The Audy Home case is, in a sense, not really planning a medical department, but instead planning how to live in one that is practically finished. This limitation would not have occurred if the medical department had initially been planned with the aid of an individual or group whose area of expertise was health facility planning and design. Unfortunately this input was lacking; had it been utilized at an early stage of the project two results would probably have been achieved: (1) the medical facility would have been substantially more functional, and (2) the facility would have been considerably less expensive.

Status of Medical Department: 1971-1972

A normal day in the Audy Home medical department begins when a full-time pediatrician starts the morning intake physical examinations of newly admitted children. These examinations, which take place in one of three well-maintained examination and treatment rooms, consist of a five-minute history and physical that includes taking a vaginal smear for girls. This same intake physical routine is repeated for newly admitted children in the late afternoon by a part-time contract physician.

Meanwhile, also in the medical department, children are brought to see the other pediatrician, who is also chief of service. Her routine includes review of medical records of complaints and the subsequent examination and treatment of these children. Medication distribution is handled by nurses throughout the day; in general, this function is well-controlled since children are brought to the department, given their medications, and, in the case of oral drugs, observed while the drugs are swallowed.

Following this initial work-up, children are again seen by the medical department where blood is drawn and a trichomona test performed for girls, and a Schick test is performed for every child.

The dental department, which has a one-chair office, had in the past done routine charting of the mouth and taken care of serious dental problems. At the time of this study, the service was not available because of the dentist's retirement.

In sum, the staffing in the department was on a 24-hour basis with seven practical and registered nurses, one chief physician, one court physician, and two contract physicians, with an intake physician present for approximately 1 to 2 hours seven days per week in the morning and 1 to 2 hours in the afternoon, and the chief physician in for 2 to 3 hours in the morning Monday to Friday and on call for the remainder of the time. Other personnel included one typist and three laboratory technicians. The 1971 budgeted payroll for this staff was $173,150.00.

Evaluation of Existing Medical Department

Medical care was found to be fragmented; that is, unrelated to medical care received elsewhere. Rarely were a child's medical records requested from another medical institution or physician, and rarely were copies of Audy Home records sent to other medical institutions. The medical history came primarily from the child—a questionably reliable source; thus, the Audy Home medical picture became a snapshot that was never considered vis-a-vis other medical episodes.

Quality control is essentially non-existent. The medical and ancillary care practiced at Audy is similiar to that received in an office. Patients are seen and treated and the cases are never evaluated or audited by peers. Furthermore, lab test results are not periodically compared for reliability with outside laboratory results.

Finally, some routine activities are of questionable value; for example, many pediatricians suggest that the Schick test (which is routinely done on every admission) is of little value. Perhaps more important, the value of routinely performed admission tests was never assessed despite review of a sample of the records which indicated that there was an annual recidivism rate of 35 to 50 percent.

The New Medical Department—Plans

The new medical department was planned as a 12,000-square-foot area in the east wing of the new steel-plated square block Audy Home and Court Building. This unit was to have:

—30 private rooms with toilet and wash basin
—two examination rooms, each room with four curtained cubicles
—two waiting rooms
—clerical and medical record space
—office space for psychologist, psychiatrist, chief physician, and nurses
—one staff and visitor waiting area
—lab space
—X-ray space
—dentist's unit
—two showers for children
—conference room
—two nursing stations
—two secure patient waiting rooms

Immediately adjacent to the spaces on the north side was to be the boys' intake unit and on the south side the girls' unit.

Traffic flow in the new medical area will be of two types, external and internal. External flow will consist primarily of new children receiving their routing examinations and Audy Home residents getting medical attention. Internal traffic will involve the treatment of children who have been transferred to the medical department sleeping area.

The architectural plans for the new facility are shown in Fig. 1.

Evaluation of New Department Plans

1. Care will be just as fragmented in the new department as in the old.

2. Storage space is lacking.

3. Only the inside corridor will be useful for patient traffic since use of the outside corridor would cause well children to disturb unnecessarily the privacy of sick children.

4. Examination cubicles lack privacy for patient-physician consultations.

5. The X-ray facility is unnecessary. The cost of building, equipping, and running an X-ray unit is exhorbitant. Justification for the unit is questionable since routine TB screening is not performed. The cost of running the unit will be high since an X-ray technician and darkroom technician will have to be hired. Furthermore, movement of an injured child to the X-ray unit may be considerably more hazardous than moving a portable X-ray to the injured child.

6. The number of patient rooms is higher than required if the rooms are to be used strictly for sick children. Statements from the medical department demonstrate that approximately 50 percent of the children in the medical section have nothing medically wrong with them but are in the ward to isolate them from other children for security or adjustment problems. This situation should be eliminated in the new Home since each child will have a private room.

National Center for Health Statistics data indicate that a population such as that at the Audy Home should for medical reasons restrict to bed five children per day and limit the activity of another seven children.

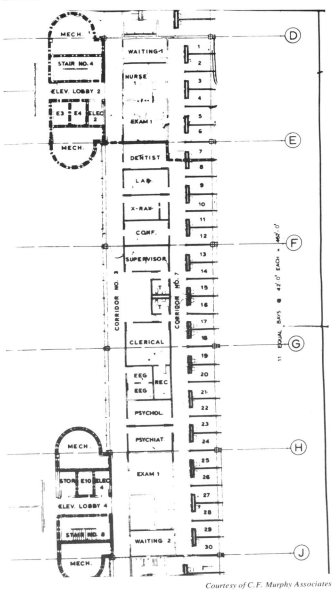

Courtesy of C.F. Murphy Associates

FIG. 1.   Medical Department, Arthur J. Audy Home, Chicago, Illinois

Specific Recommendations

It was the consultant's opinion that the present medical department has some serious shortcomings that should be rectified and that the new medical department is less than optimally designed. Recommendations for solution of these problems are divided into two categories—functional recommendations and design recommendations.

Functional Recommendations

1. The medical department at the Audy Home should be eliminated. In its place the administration of the Home should enter into a specific performance contract with the Cook County Hospital Commission for comprehensive pediatric services for the Home's residents. Specifically:

> The department of pediatrics of Cook County Hospital should be responsible for delivering a complete range of medical services to children at the Home. Included in this package would be complete physicals, preventative care, emergency care, routine and in-patient care. Facilities for out-patient medical care should continue to be provided at the Audy Home. This contract should be monitored for quality by the Cook County Department of Health. Its administrative enforcement should be by the Superintendent of the Audy Home.

A contractual arrangement would have the following net effect:

It should cost less to operate than the present medical department because

a. Supplies and drugs will be purchased at considerable savings through the Cook County Hospital.

b. More hours of physician medical care will be available for the same dollars.

c. Duplication of testing will be eliminated—medical data will be available for many children that is presently not available.

d. Referral to out-patient clinics and other ancillary services will be expedited.

2. Until such time as recommendation 1 is put into effect it is strongly suggested that a medical advisory board be appointed, consisting of individuals such as the Chief of Pediatrics, Cook County Hospital, the Chairman of the Pediatrics Department,

University of Illinois College of Medicine, and the Chairman of the Pediatrics Department, University of Chicago Medical School. This board would review medical procedures and function as a general mechanism for maintaining quality control. The lack of such a control mechanism may make the Audy Home and its medical staff more vulnerable to litigation than if a review mechanism existed.

    3. The present medical staff should be placed on an hourly salary with a special fee for telephone consultations. At present, considerable savings could be effected if this plan were adopted.

    4. The present medical department should be able to function effectively in the new medical department. No new staff is necessary.

Design Recommendations (The New Home)

    1. Two children's rooms at each end of the medical area should be redesigned for physician's offices. These rooms should have desks, two chairs, an examining light, and file cabinets. The rooms should be used for physician-patient interviewing and counseling. The present plan does not allow for private interviewing and counseling nor does it allow for private physician space. Elimination of the rooms should in no way affect the ability of the medical department to meet its goals.

    2. Each of the two exam rooms should make one of its four cubicles into a blood drawing area. This will eliminate considerable traffic in the corridor—it will be easier to have one laboratory technician go to the various blood drawing rooms than to have a dozen people moving through what could be a congested corridor with a consequent security problem.

    3. The X-ray should be eliminated. X-rays are not only expensive to purchase (the machine ordered costs over $12,000.00) but their operational expenses are high; that is, the services of X-ray technicians and darkroom technicians will cost in excess of $20,000.00 per year. Perhaps more important, a permanently installed machine is of dubious value. As an alternative it is suggested that a small portable X-ray with an instant developing attachment be purchased. Such a machine can be used in any part of the building without special shielding. This type of X-ray does not require a darkroom technician; nurses can be trained to operate it, and, most important, an injured child does not have to be moved to

be X-rayed. The result is minimization of the risk of exacerbating the injury through movement.

4. The conference room should be divided in half. One half should be made a staff locker room, and the other section should remain a conference area. The present locker room is a considerable distance from the medical department, and time will be lost that could be otherwise utilized for change of shift reports, patient care, or patient record keeping.

5. The supervisor's room should be divided in half—one half (the room opening on the inner corridor) should remain the supervisor's office, and the other half should be used for bulk storage—a definite need that is not presently designed into the department.

Discussion

This case demonstrates the difficulty of planning in an ongoing operating situation. Clearly, the building program had developed its own momentum with staff and administration quite committed to change as they had planned it. Indeed, the consultant had the distinct impression that his role was not "to reason why" but simply to justify.

The consultant's recommendations were considered but not accepted, the new Home opened in October 1973, and changes in the basic medical program did not occur. Whether such changes would have come about with earlier consultation in view of the value of the recommended changes is a matter for speculation.

CHAPTER 6

Orleans Parish Prison—
"Cruel and Unusual Punishment"

In the fall of 1974 a group of public health professionals who were members of the American Public Health Association's Task Force on Prisons and Jails toured the medical department of Orleans Parish Prison in New Orleans, Louisiana. What they found was a modern, clean, well-staffed and equipped facility which, despite a number of deficiencies, seemed to provide inmates with comprehensive care of good quality. Had they visited the medical department three years earlier, they would have found a different picture, as described in this chapter.

Basic information came from the literature on prison medicine, from official reports and correspondence relating to the Orleans Parish Prison's medical system, and from interviews with State government officials, prison officials, prison medical and custodial personnel, and inmates. Additional data were taken from consultative reports written by a medical records librarian, two pharmacists, and a nutritionist; from a review of a sample of the medical records at the parish prison; from an epidemiologic survey of a sample of inmates at this prison—information which included detailed histories and the results of physical examinations; and finally, from systematic observation at the prison over a two-month period.

Class Action Suit for Inmates

The first in a series of events that led to the establishment of a new system of medical care at the Orleans Parish Prison was a class action suit *(Louis Hamilton, et al. V. Victor Schiro, et al.).* This suit was filed in October 1969 against the City of New Orleans, its mayor, city council, criminal sherriff, and the Orleans Parish Prison warden on behalf of the inmates at the Orleans Parish Prison. The court agreed with the inmates' allegations that conditions at the prison constituted cruel and unusual punishment in violation of the Eighth Amendment of the Constitution of the

United States. Following are some of the improtant findings of fact by the judge that related to the medical care system of the prison:[1]

> The danger of an outbreak of contagious diseases is great as a result of the unsanitary conditions in the toilets, the kitchen and sleeping equipment. Further, no medical intake survey is made to detect prisoners with contagious diseases. Although the incidence of gonorrhea is high, only sporadic blood tests for syphilis are done. As a result of the crowded conditions, there is no isolation or quarantine area for those with contagious diseases that are detected.
>
> The combined effects of the fearful atmosphere and crowded and sordid living conditions has a severe effect on psychotics, often causing those transferred to the prison from mental hospitals to be returned to the hospitals. Disruptive psychotic prisoners are sometime moved into a hallway by the main gate and shackled to the bars.
>
> Hospital facilities and medical attention are woefully inadequate to meet the needs of the inmates. Inmates who should be confined to bed with chronic diseases must be kept on the open tiers. Medication that is prescribed frequently never reaches the inmate or else is taken from him by other prisoners.

As a result of the litigation, a judicial order was issued directing the defendants to correct immediately the deficiencies enumerated in the suit. A year passed, however, without much discernible improvement in the parish prison.

Finally, in Ocotober 1971, two years after the original petition was filed, the Federal Court appointed a federal special master to investigate and formulate a reasonable and effective plan for correcting the prison's deficiencies. (Special masters, usually attorneys, are judicially appointed; they serve the courts as fact finders or referees in complex civil cases, but their use is infrequent. Appointment of a special master in the type of civil rights case described was considered to be an important legal innovation.)

Because of the obvious health needs delineated by the judge, the federal special master Robert Force made medical care his first area of concern. Since, however, health systems were not his area of expertise, the author was appointed health care consultant to the project and was deputized with the same broad investigatory powers as the master. In this consultative role the author prepared the medical care section of the master's report and formulated plans for changing the health care delivery system at the prison.

Process of Medical Care at Prison

Conceptually, medical care in the 40-year-old dirty and poorly ventilated Orleans Parish Prison appeared to be rationally organized and reasonably operated. The breakdowns that occurred in the system, however, suggested an alternative hypothesis.

The new inmate's first encounter with the prison's medical system was in the docks, where between 15 and 35 men shared an open jail cell while awaiting the magistrate's arraignment. Here, using the daily intake report sheet, an inmate-trustee administered, without explanation, a tuberculin skin test (tine). If one to two days later the person tested was still in prison and could be located, the inmate-trustee would read the test. Positive results led to a chest X-ray's being taken, which was subsequently read by the tuberculosis control staff of the city health department. When the prison's X-ray machine was not operative (as was the case for the last six months of 1971), the health department sent over portable equipment and an operator on a weekly basis.

The inmate's second encounter with the medical system occurred in the booking room after his hearing when the booking officer asked each new inmate, "Is your health good?" or "Is your health good or bad?" The response was duly recorded on the back of the booking card. When a person was obviously in distress or stated a seemingly serious complaint, he was immediately referred to the nurse or physician for treatment.

After assignment to a cell and tier, an inmate could request emergency treatment at any time and routine care at specified times through a variety of mechanisms. The most popular method of getting medical attention was to place one's name on the medical sheet that was circulated by an inmate-trustee (hallboy) or deputy and transmitted to the nurse. A second popular way was to have a hallboy or deputy act as spokesman for the inmate seeking treatment and tell his "story" to the nurse, or in the case of the deputy, get him to actually bring the inmate down to see the nurse or physician. Writing a note or seeing the warden or associate warden, as well as bringing some outside pressure from the folks at home, would sometimes result in an inmate's getting medical attention. Finally, in an emergency or from utter frustration, the inmate could resort to the "beat down" or "knock down"—when the inmates on one or more tiers begin beating simultaneously on the bars—to attract attention.

Breakdowns in the medical care system with these methods were identifiable, numerous, and often horrendous. Specifically, the author's discussions with staff and inmates indicated that prisoners sometimes had to "pay off" hallboys and, indeed, even deputies, to get their names on the list. Furthermore, once the list got to the nurse, a determination as to whether to see or not to see the inmate would be made on the basis of a subjective assessment of the complainant and the nature of the stated complaint. Obviously, the more articulate and prison-wise the hallboy or the inmate, the more likely was the inmate to get medical attention. When deputies brought inmates for care, custodial problems arose; the tier was left unattended and staff relations became strained— the medical people thinking the deputies were trying to break the monotony of tier work and "goof-off" by bringing someone to the prison hospital and the deputies thinking that if the medical personnel only did their job, the deputies would not have to waste their time bringing inmates to the hospital. Finally, the "knockdown" was used so often that everyone responded slowly to these calls, and the effectiveness of this emergency signaling system was thereby diminished.

The fourth stage in the medical process was that of specialty care, which was provided at Charity Hospital. After a determination by the part-time physician at Orleans Parish Prison (12 hours per week) or the only full-time nurse (40 hours per week—no holidays, weekends, or nights) that an inmate needed some type of specialized care, the inmate and a deputy would go to the hospital and make an appointment. On the day of the appointment, the inmate (legs and hands shackled) and the deputy were sent to the hospital again for the visit. If possible, appointments made by inmates before their incarceration were kept. Generally, however, for security reasons, to prevent the planning of an escape, inmates were not told in advance of their appointment dates. Since there was no prison ward at Charity Hospital, admission meant placement in the general ward. Security of an inmate who was an inpatient at Charity Hospital was handled by shackling him to his bed and thereafter having him checked by the three-man patrol of armed deputies assigned full-time to the hospital. All inmates with serious medical problems which arose after hours and on weekends were transferred to Charity Hospital for care.

Dental care, consisting entirely of extractions, was provided one evening a week. Inmates requested this service by signing a dental sheet, and here again the logistics of assembling the inmates from two outlying buildings and the various prison tiers sometimes precluded their obtaining the necessary care.

Quality of Care at Prison

Although measuring the quality of medical care is difficult, there are some widely accepted minimal standards of good practice, such as those set by the Joint Commission on the Accreditation of Hospitals and by the federal and state governments for Medicare and Medicaid facilities, as well as the common standards of practice of most medical practitioners. Unfortunately, the work performed at the parish prison did not meet any of these standards.

For example, minimal standards of practice require the maintenance of adequate medical records that will provide information on a patient's medical history, health status, disabilities, diseases, treatments, and treatment results. The medical record is the narrative that documents the various encounters a person has with the health care delivery system and, if properly maintained, it has considerable medical as well as legal importance.

In a review of the medical records of the prison for September 1971, it was found that, in almost all instances, an adequate medical history had not been taken, nor had a physical examination or laboratory work-up been done. Furthermore, although the medical records indicated that a treatment had been given, almost 25 percent did not show a diagnosis; 42 percent of the records were not signed so that the individual who had treated the inmate could not be identified. The most prevalent medical problems were minor traumatic injuries, dermatological difficulties, and venereal disease:

Medical problem	Number of inmates
Injuries, stabbings, lacerations	76
Dermatological conditions	25
Venereal disease	23
Stomach ailments	17
Colds	14
Nervousness	12
Eye irritation	11
Suture removal	10
Pregnancy	8

Under the system in force, it was not until an inmate had his first encounter with the medical system—possibly days or months after being jailed—that his previous medical treatment was for the first time discussed and a request made for his records. It is perhaps of greater significance that, even when good historical data were available, they were not used. For example, during the course of the author's study, arrangements were made for community medicine students to take medical histories and perform routine physical examinations on incoming inmates under the supervision of a physician. Once these data were collected, however, and turned over to the prison medical department, they were filed and never used. The attitude of the medical department staff might be best characterized as that of a "quick fix" approach—responsibility was abdicated for virtually any type of treatment that required followup or monitoring.

Adequate quality care presupposes the existence of some minimal equipment, such as a scale and examining table—two basic pieces of equipment that the prison hospital did not possess. The total complement of reference books available to the nurse was one—the free give-away drug book, the PDR (Physician's Desk Reference). Nowhere in sight were such potentially valuable books for the nurse as the Merck Manual or a medical dictionary. Indeed, in terms of delivering adequate medical care, it would have been better to spend less money on the superficial accouterments of an office, such as a carpet, and more on needed basic equipment, reference materials, and first aid equipment—the hospital did not even have a plastic airway or Ambu-bag.

The author's observation of the physician's practice was limited. Clearly, while both the physician and the nurse were hamstrung by a lack of resources to examine and treat, they did not use the resources they had. For example, although agreements had been made with the health department and Charity Hospital to perform laboratory work, blood or urine samples were rarely sent out for examination, and only on rare occasions was urine tested by the "dip-stick" method.

Followup of patients is another basic element in care, and here again the prison medical system fell short of the mark. The major part of the difficulty was logistical; that is, the medical staff was never sure when an emergency might arise, when the physician would come in, or when an inmate would be able to get off the tier. Here there were really two problems—custodial functions superseded medical functions, and the medical department was poorly administered, as exemplified by the fact that a great many inmates were told ". . . wait and we will have you see the doctor"—some medical records indeed bore the notation "to see Dr.—" but the physician was rarely seen.

Next, there was the problem of drugs, legal ones. Fifteen percent of the prisoners were continuously on mood-changing drugs. Eighty-five percent of the inmates' contacts with the jail medical system during September 1971 resulted in their getting at least one of the following:

Item	Times prescribed
Tetracycline	87
Bacitracin, boric acid, Desenex ointment	64
Vanquish	37
Nasal spray, cough syrup	35
Phisohex	30
Multi-vitamins	26
Valium, Librium	17
Polysporin ointment	17
Percogesic	17

The followup of patients for whom drugs were prescribed, the taking of histories of their previous reactions to drugs, and the administration of appropriate treatment for adverse reactions were virtually unknown at the Orleans Parish Prison. For example, during one of the author's visits to the prison an inmate had a grand mal seizure because he was taking the wrong drug. The prison did not have the injectable drugs needed to treat him after the seizure, nor did the nurse know the appropriate treatment. In fact she did not plan to treat the inmate at all, but was prodded into action by an outside physician, who happened to be touring the jail at the time.

The nurse's answer to the problem was that "Charity Hospital is only three minutes down the street." While her statement was indeed correct, 30 minutes to an hour were lost in getting the inmate from the fourth floor prison hospital ward to the first floor examining room, onto a stretcher, into a vehicle, and to Charity Hospital. More important, perhaps, the whole difficulty might have been avoided had a proper work-up been done initially. The man had been booked into prison on a Thursday with only one complaint listed in respect to his physical condition—"bad eyes." His medical abstract was not sent for until the following Monday, when he had come to the prison medical department to complain of head pains.

Finally, there was the question of psychiatric care for the inmates. It was essentially nonexistent. Inmates with serious psychiatric problems were sent to Charity Hospital. Sometimes they were kept there; at other times they were sent back to the prison, where they were either tranquilized with drugs or shackled to bars near the main entrance.

In summary, while the limited resources circumscribed the medical department's ability to provide the highest quality care, the resources that were present were poorly used, and the result was care that was not even minimally adequate. Fortunately for all concerned, the inmate population of the parish prison—while great complainers—was basically made up of healthy young people who seemingly could stand being incarcerated without proper medical care.

In a special study of 50 inmates in December 1971, no major medical problems were found on gross physical examination, although, as can be seen in the following table, a large percentage of the 50 inmates complained of a variety of conditions. Basic laboratory work-ups, moreover, presented information suggesting that 14 percent might have had an active venereal disease and that 14 percent might have had a urinary tract infection. A review of the available medical records of these inmates showed that none had been seen previously for either type of infection. Perhaps of greater significance was the observation that two weeks after the abnormal results of tests had been returned to the prison hospital, none of the inmates to whom they pertained had received either followup laboratory work or treatment.

Medical condition	Percentage
Frequent trouble sleeping	69
Dizziness or fainting spells	57
Nervous trouble of any sort	53
Depression or excessive worry	51
Pain or pressure in chest	45
Frequent or severe headaches	45
Venereal disease—syphilis, gonorrhea, and so forth	45
Leg cramps	41
Head injury	37
Severe tooth or gum trouble	37
Shortness of breath	35
Fractures	35
Eye trouble	31
Chronic or frequent colds	31
Palpitation or pounding heart	29
Recurrent back pain	29

Quantity of Care at Prison

There was considerable discrepancy between the officially stated amount of medical care available at the parish prison and the amount revealed by observation, interviews with inmates, and a review of the medical records. According to official reports and statements of the prison nurse and physician, an average of 800 inmates per month were seen by the nurse and 500 by the physician. The other sources, however, clearly indicated that only 500 inmates per month were seen by the nurse and 180 by the physician.

The total staff available to deliver the care comprised one physician working approximately 12 hours per week on an unscheduled basis; one full-time nurse; three deputy sheriffs, who delivered and dispensed drugs and provided inmate transportation to Charity Hospital but rarely provided first aid or medical assistance; several inmates who performed recordkeeping functions and general "runner" activities, such as escorting other inmates back and forth from locked tiers; and a full-time salaried pharmacist, who worked 10 to 15 hours per week filling prescriptions. Care was provided in the one-room medical department, a room which was used for both clerical work and physical examinations. An eight-bed prison hospital ward located four floors away was used as a self-care unit for convalescing inmates. The patients on this unit, who were basically under the control of a hospital trustee-inmate, were rarely checked by the nurse or physician more than once every several weeks.

Dental care, consisting almost entirely of extractions, was also available at the prison. Once a week a dentist came to the prison to extract teeth. Officially, an average of 17 extractions were performed each week, and an average of 46 inmates per week were seen under the dental program (exclusive of referrals to Charity Hospital for extractions of wisdom teeth). One dentist reported, however, that approximately 20 patients per week were seen, and worksheet reports indicated a weekly average of 11 visits and 9.2 extractions—significantly below the officially reported 46 visits and 17 extractions. The reported working hours of the dentists, of between two and three hours per week, appeared to be accurate. The fee for these two to three hour sessions was $100, or $35 to $50 per hour (net).

A New Approach

This study demonstrated that the Orleans Parish Prison's medical department was unable to deliver a minimally acceptable quantity and quality of health care to inmates. This result was not completely unexpected. The job entrusted to the medical department was frustrating and, indeed, often unstimulating. The atmosphere was difficult, and the relationships between the professional staff of the medical department, the group of jail deputies, and the prison administration was strained at best. This conflict was natural and to be expected since the custodial goals of a jailhouse conflict with the therapeutic goals of a medical department.

Who suffers because of the problems described?—inmates, 80 to 85 percent of whom are in jail not because they have been convicted of any crime but rather because they are awaiting trial and cannot afford bond.

The author's proposed solution to these problems was to con-tract for medical services outside the jail. The author recom-mended, and the court ordered, that the Orleans Parish Prison enter into a specific performance contract with an appropriately qualified medical group to deliver medical services to Orleans Parish prisoners. Under this plan, administrative authority was to be retained by the criminal sheriff, professional responsibility was to be placed in the hands of the contracting group, and the City of New Orleans Health Department was to be given responsibility for monitoring the quality of medical care provided. Basically, the contractor agreed to perform routine intake physical examinations and conduct routine sick call for all inmates on a 24-hour basis. In addition, the contractor agreed to provide comprehensive back-up consultative services—medical, surgical obstetrical, and psychiatric—and also emergency medical services; medications were to be ordered on a cost basis. The contractee (the Orleans Parish Prison and the City of New Orleans) agreed to provide ap-propriate physical space, equipment, and supplies and to reim-burse the contractor for services of medical and nonmedical personnel and supplies.

This approach, while drastic, seemed to be necessary if a reasonable quality and quantity of care was to be delivered to the parish prison inmates. Clearly, the medical department and the inmates' medical problems were a headache for the prison ad-mininstration. This approach for the first time caused the payers of care and the providers of care to sit down and spell out what they wanted from each other. Moreover, with a clear delineation of responsibility and authority, everyone for the first time knew what his job was vis-a-vis medical care.

To Charity Hospital (or indeed to any other medical group such as the medical schools of Tulane University or Louisiana State University), the contract would mean primarily an excellent clinical experience for its house staff and, secondarily, a way to make some money.

Such a program is expensive at $138,000 per year. Its cost represents an increase of 100 percent over the medical depart-ment's previous budget. This added money, however, will provide 24-hour instead of 8-hour coverage; 50 hours of physician time per week instead of 12; and complete laboratory work-ups, including

SMA 12 (AutoAnalyzer) determinations and urinalyses, instead of no laboratory work—in short, comprehensive medical care where relatively little has previously existed.

Charity Hospital is now delivering the medical care to the Orleans Parish Prison inmates. The task of the Federal Court with respect to the prison is not yet finished; still to be addressed are the significant questions of the organization and internal management of the prison and the work flow of the criminal courts. Finally, the Federal Court, the City of New Orleans Health Department, and Charity Hospital must engage in a careful evaluation of the new medical system, but it appears to be an important positive step toward alleviating the abysmal medical conditions uncovered by the author's study.

Appendix: Consultative Reports

November 18, 1971

Memo To: Study Director

From: Medical Record Consultant

Subject: Medical Records at Orleans Parish Prison

On Friday, November 12, 1971, I had the opportunity to examine the medical records at the Orleans Parish Prison. The prison's clinic functions like an outpatient clinic with Charity Hospital as the provider of inpatient care. Therefore, the medical records should contain, at least, the following:

(1) proper patient identification

(2) dates of visits

(3) chief complaint

(4) observations (temperature, blood pressure, rashes, etc.)

(5) impression or diagnosis

(6) treatment and/or disposition

(7) signatures (i.e., M.D., R.N., Pharmacists, etc.)

Omission of one or more of these items may have very serious medical-legal implications. More important is that an incomplete, inaccurate medical record may affect the quality of care delivered to the patient.

Upon reviewing the prison records, I found that patient identification in general was good. There were a few records on which the age, race, or middle initial (or name) was omitted. An expected problem in such institutions is the use of aliases. Not one of the records I examined referred to a record of the same inmate under another name (i.e., cross references).

The date was consistently entered on all records examined but I found the form itself (i.e., 5 × 7 cards) inadequate in format and difficult to work with when a number of cards were needed for one patient.

The chief complaint is very important for medical-legal reasons and should be recorded in the patient's own words. On most records there was no chief complaint or observations. A number of the medical records did have a diagnosis or an impression but the majority did not. Treatment and/or disposition (i.e., to Charity Hospital) was recorded on most records but without a chief complaint, diagnosis or impression, this would mean very little in a court of law.

The absence of signatures on most medical records renders them useless as evidence and undermines the communicative intent of medical records among the different medical disciplines.

In summary, a complete medical record must contain sufficient written data to justify the diagnosis and warrant the treatment and end results. The medical records at the Orleans Parish Prison, in my opinion, are grossly inadequate according to generally accepted criteria for outpatient medical records.

December 1, 1971

Memo To: Study Director

From: Consultant Pharmacist

Subject: Report on Pharmacy Service in Parish Prison

The pharmacy in Parish Prison is extremely limited in space and equipment. These physical limitations do not, however, severely constrict the scope of the service which may be offered.

Pharmacy in an institution should be concerned with all aspects of medication including procurement, storage, dispensing, distribution, and administration. The pharmacy service in the prison will be evaluated below in each of these areas.

Procurement—While no records were available to substantiate generic purchasing, the stock on hand and prices quoted by the pharmacist indicate that all reasonable steps to procure items as economically as possible were being used.

Storage—Because physical space is at a premium, storage should be accomplished in as orderly a process as possible. Medications were stored in two cabinets. No recognizable pattern of shelving was seen. Two containers of the same medication were shelved at different locations. Both containers were open and partially used. While no containers having medication which was out of date were found, no system of segregation of dated merchandise to prevent dispensing of expired medication was used. A refrigerator was available for storage of refrigerated items but no thermometer was in the refrigerator.

Dispensing—A very unsatisfactory procedure for dispensing of medications was used:

(a) No prescriptions for the medication dispensed were on hand in the pharmacy. No records of any type were available to indicate who ordered the medication for a patient, how much was dispensed, or how much medication was given by refill. When asked where the prescriptions for the medication were the pharmacist replied that when he filled the prescription he returned it to the nurse. (Later when the trustee in the infirmary was questioned about this he said that all prescriptions were in the pharmacy). When questioned as to how he knew a physician ordered the medication for the patient, the pharmacist said that the nurse orders the majority of the medications but that the doctor checks and O.K.'s what she has done.

(b) The observed procedure for filling the prescriptions was both extremely dangerous and unsanitary. A sufficient quantity for the next dose only was dispensed which is very good but the method used to fill the container was very poor. Envelopes were filled from several small, unlabeled bins containing medication. Selection was made by recognition of color/size/shape and by a non-pharmacist volunteer. No counting trays or other system to attempt to improve sanitation was used. Each tablet/capsule was grasped by hand and placed in the envelope.

Distribution of the medication to the patients was done by several of the prison personnel. A new system which utilized a single guard on morning and evening shifts was initiated while I was there but only for one day prior to this report—evaluation of this cannot be done. The attempt to try to improve distribution, however, is the only incidence of an effort to improvise and improve any aspect of the pharmacy.

Administration is usually the concern of individuals other than the pharmacist but it is certainly within his area of concern. Nothing to indicate any effort by the pharmacist to improve the current system was seen. Currently medication is administered by the guards on the cell blocks. No records of administration are maintained.

December 1, 1971

Memo To: Study Director

From: Registered Pharmacist

Subject: Evaluation of Pharmacy
               Orleans Parish Prison

The pharmacy, like other facilities at Parish Prison is grossly inadequate. The shortcomings, in some cases, have a direct and negative effect on medical care of the inmates.

Prescriptions are sometimes being filled by a non-registered person who is not under the direct supervision of a pharmacist.

The "automatic refill" system could be causing great harm to the patients. A large percentage, 91%, of the 112 prisoners whose precriptions were sampled are taking tranquilizers. Many of these patients are taking them at dosage levels which require direct observation by a physician and monitoring for side effects. Some dosage levels also indicate that some inmates should receive psychiatric treatment and/or isolation.

The number as well as the types of drugs stocked is very limited. As mentioned previously, there is a great reliance on psychotherapeutic drugs. More antibiotic, dermatological, analgesic and vitamin supplement drugs should be stocked.

There should be a greater degree of coordination between the pharmacist and doctor(s). This problem cannot be solved until more physician time is available for the inmates who are in need of attention. Preferably, the doctor should be available to authorize a specific number of refills after checking patients' conditions.

The drug distribution system needs improvement. Perhaps each tier's prescriptions could be filled and placed in a locked box. All boxes could then be delivered via a locked drug cart. This could eliminate some of the problems with missing prescriptions. Only the guard would have a key to the tier's drug box. Only the pharmacist would have a key to the drug cart.

In all fairness to the staff, it is recognized that the drug room is entirely too small to permit orderly arrangement and work flow. Some unsanitary work habits, however, could be improved.

There is little that can be done to improve pharmacy service with existing patterns. employees and facilities. Funding too needs better management or increasing. Even changing all four of these factors inside the pharmacy will not result in vast improvement in the health of inmates without more physician or paramedical involvement. Without physicians, there can be no pharmacist; without physician services, only insufficient pharmaceutical service can result.

Memorandum To: Study Director

From: Physician/Nutritionist Consultant

Re: Visit to Parish Prison

Thank you for your time and courtesy last Friday, December 3, 1971, in showing me the medical facilities at the New Orleans Parish Prison. I am sending you this summary of my impressions.

The visit began with a stop at the clinic at approximately 9:30 a.m. No medical personnel were present, but a deputy and inmate were discussing the inmate's condition. He was complaining of inability to sleep the preceding night and thought that since his medication for his epilepsy had been abruptly changed from phenobarbital and Dilantin to Mysoline a few days previous, he was not feeling well. He gave the history of a previous trial of Mysoline at Veterans Hospital that was not therapeutically successful. Review of his prison medical chart gave no history or physical exam data. He was told to wait for the nurse who was due in soon.

Approximately one hour later, the patient was next seen in status epilepticus, being carried from his cell area back down to the clinic. There was considerable confusion because available elevators were being used for food service. I next saw him in the clinic area where the seizure activity had not diminished. The nurse was in attendance. No mouthpiece was inserted due to clenched jaw and the personnel were discussing whether to shackle him as he lay on a wire stretcher. No medications had been given and on inquiry from the nurse, there are no medications available in the clinic to treat such a medical emergency.

From this case observation several recommendations can be proposed:

(1) Institute equipment and medical supplies to handle this emergency as well as other acute medical emergencies. (Exintravenous Valium and/or phenobarbital, plastic airways, at least hand suction bulbs to handle secretions, Ambu bag for artificial respiration.)

(2) Adequate and prompt transfer of medical records on patients seen at hospitals, especially for management of chronic diseases.

(3) Medical history and physical exam on inmates with special attention to those under medical supervision prior to incarceration. A visit to the hospital area of the jail introduced four inmates:

(a) The first was a man claiming to be 91 years of age, watching television alone in a room. He had no medical complaints and was awaiting imminent release from prison.

(b) The second was a man recovering from gunshot wounds. He was doing well.

(c) The third was another case recuperating from gunshot wounds.

(d) The last was an out-of-state man awaiting trial for the past three months with a broken leg. He was mending well, except for cough and low-grade fever at night. The fourth case had had a chest film read as "negative" for tuberculosis although he said that he had not been skin tested for the disease. No further work-up of the fever had been attempted.

A tour of the kitchen facility revealed a clean, modern set-up. A list of menus provided by the warden showed adequate nutritional food provided to inmates. Several of the inmates complained of loss of appetite and weakness. This is more probably secondary to monotony of the menu and personal depression rather than adequate nutritional requirements supplied. It was suggested that the warden use the excellent consulting service provided by the Louisiana State Nutrition Section under Miss Roseann Langham located here in New Orleans.

Although isolated cases may lend themselves to more specific medical care evaluation, the more generalized conditions observed throughout the prison contribute more to the physical and mental illness prevalent in the general prison population. On this specific chilly day, inmates were observed weaving newspaper through the window frames devoid of glass. The dark, crowded conditions in several cell block areas were ideal for spawning the daily outbreaks of prison violence recounted by the warden. The rehabilitation section of the prison revealed a section of locked doors except for a small, open library being utilized by several inmates.

I thank you again for the opportunity to be of assistance to you and hope that medical care improvement would be a first step in generating attention to this serious problem of prison conditions.

Reference

[1] *Louis Hamilton, et al., V. Victor Shiro, et al.* U.S. Dist. Ct., Eastern Dist., La., New Orleans Div., Case No. 69-2443, pp. 3-5.

Part 3

Vignettes

CHAPTER 7

Inmates, Correctional and Medical Staff

This chapter presents eighteen vignettes of inmates, correctional staff, and medical staff who are all in various ways caught up in the web of prison health.

These portraits, based on composites of real people, display a picture that is replete with desperation, boredom, despair—and occasionally hope.

They speak for themselves.

Inmates

> *Jack*
> *Coco*
> *Irwin*
> *Billy*
> *Max*
> *Shakespeare*
> *Flash*

Jack

Twenty percent of Jack's life was spent behind bars as an inmate. His career as a criminal began at 19 with an arrest for narcotics possession. At the time he was in the Navy and also a drug addict. With conviction on the narcotics charge he was discharged from the Navy and sent to the Federal Center at Fort Worth for heroin withdrawal. Six months later he was discharged.

For four years he worked as a salesman for a small automobile parts company in El Paso. He did well and enjoyed his financial success, spending his money on atuomobiles, women, and gambling. These almost insatiable desires led him into the more lucrative business of selling narcotics. He again became a drug addict, and, recognizing his plight, he voluntarily checked himself back into the Federal Narcotic Rehabilitation Center at Lexington, Kentucky.

Four months later he was out and living in Houston where, for the next few years, he worked steadily and successfully as a used car salesman. He had developed stable relationships, stayed drug free, and started a self-education program which was encouraged by the woman with whom he lived, a school teacher.

After two years his relationship with the teacher ended when, one day, he returned from work to find that she had left him. Depression hit Jack hard, and he sought solace in drugs and liquor. His appetites grew, and he needed a new source of income.

This time he hit upon a novel idea. He married a wealthy woman whom he met at a singles bar, in the hope of becoming a bit more affluent. It didn't quite work out, because her parents found out about Jack's past and cut her off financially and spiritually.

Appparently this came as a significant shock to her, and she then started on a program of rehabilitating Jack. The degree to which he was interested in rehabilitation is a matter for some speculation, since he started drinking and drugging more heavily. The cost of these various habits and the desire to show his wife how well he was doing as a used car salesman caused him to return to his old line of selling drugs. One of his buyers, a police officer, arrested him.

Plea bargaining is the process of pleading guilty to the same or a lesser offense with the understanding that the judge is going to go easy on sentencing. This was the route that Jack selected after his arrest. It got him three and a half years in a large local jail.

As an inmate a marvelous gift of gab and a pleasing personality gained him a good job within the jail and, within a year and a half, he was ready to be sent out to a halfway house where he could take a job and sleep in a supervised non-institutional environment. Within a week and a half of being on the street he had found his wife, begged for and received forgiveness, and committed himself to the straight and narrow. To celebrate his decision and his new-found partial freedom, he and his wife went night clubing. The following morning Jack realized that he had spent more money than he could afford. He felt terrible and became very depressed.

His reaction to the depression was not atypical; that is, he went out and sought amphetamines. Shortly thereafter he was caught with the drugs and returned to prison. During the next few months, significant changes occurred in Jack's personality. He became interested in transactional analysis, the "I'm OK, you're OK" approach; he became active in prison self-help groups, and he talked about himself with new insights. His sentence was completed and he left the prison. With some help from former car salesmen friends, he got a job as a salesman for a large automobile firm in town. He had long talks with his wife and they decided to have another try. They took a new apartment, and Jack started investigating the possibilities of entering college.

However, a fight with his wife led him into a period of depression. Counseling prevented the use of some drugs, but eventually Jack found that the bottle and the amphetamine pills were stronger than the talk. Where is he now? What is he doing? Nobody knows.

Coco

Coco was doing six months for assault and battery, though he didn't seem the assaulting type. He was 48, a slender West Indian, and a pharmacist.

He was from Detroit and he had been visiting the bars and nightspots of the town when, after having a bit too much to drink, he got into a fight with another patron. This ended in Coco's taking out a large knife and stabbing the other man without severely injuring him.

Coco was extremely popular among the many inmates and seemed to have the run of the institution. His work assignment was as an orderly in the prison's medical department.

The last time I saw him, Coco was cowering in the corner of the Warden's office pleading for his life. He had been threatened by three inmates who had decided to kill him because he had raised the price of the drugs he was stealing from the pharmacy.

Irwin

He couldn't believe that he was in jail. He spent the first three days and nights feeling numb—trying to think that he was really not there, that it was all a bad dream.

The bad dream started a week before in Chicago when he had a fight with his wife and he decided to go south for a long weekend. He checked into the best hotel in town, and arranged with the bellhop for a call girl. She came with a mutually agreed-upon price tag.

The following morning he woke up to find his watch and wallet missing. That afternoon he encountered the woman on a busy downtown street and demanded his money back. She claimed not to know him and when he grabbed her she screamed for help. He beat her severely (no one intervened, although a large crowd was watching) and when police sirens were heard he ran back to his room at the hotel.

Deciding that it was wise to leave town, he started to check out; however, since he had checked in under an assumed name and had no cash and no credit cards, he tried to bluff it through by writing a blank check under his assumed name on a bank in Chicago. A suspicious manager called the police who, it turned out, had been searching for a man fitting his description for the assault.

The case mounted up simply because he didn't want to identify himself. He had no identification and he didn't want to involve his wife in this matter because he was still disgusted with his home situation in Chicago. For the offenses of passing a bad check and of assault, he was given six months in jail.

Two weeks before, Irwin had been a junior account executive with a large advertising agency in Chicago, earning $20,000 a year. Now he was an inmate in a county jail making less than 20¢ an hour.

A big man, over six foot two, and weighing close to 190 pounds, he was very much concerned about his physical survival. The correctional officer had assigned him to a hostile tier group and he was terrified of going to sleep at night. He managed to speak to the chaplain in the Crisis Center and was assigned as the chaplain's assistant, which also gave him the privilege of sleeping on the floor in the chaplain's office.

Irwin had, at 32, built one life and ruined one life. He was rather uncertain as to what he would do with his next life.

Billy

Fifty-two-year-old Billy was being held on a murder charge. He had allegedly murdered a man in a bar after feuding with him, because, he claimed, the man had been running around with Billy's 23-year-old wife, a hostess in the bar.

Billy asserted that his main concern was for his two-year-old son who, he felt, was being neglected by his wife. He also felt that the whole system was against him since "half the cops on the beat were screwing my wife."

His constant threats of suicide and his constant animation called for medical intervention. Indeed, the medical department found a solution to his problems that was not particularly unique in the nineteenth century but somewhat disconcerting in the twentieth century: They filled him with tranquilizers and shackled his legs and arms to the bars.

Max

Max was being held for bail on a forgery-burglary charge.

At 28, Max was a mess. He had broken both his legs and arms in a parachuting accident several years ago and had great difficulty in walking. When he came into prison, he alleged that he was a clinical psychologist and that this whole matter was a big mistake. His mother, he pointed out, would shortly be coming in from a neighboring state and bailing him out. He had never been in trouble, he said, and he just didn't know how such a bad thing could happen to him.

In addition, he said that he was totally frightened of jails and could something be arranged; after all, he was a "doctor."

Responding to his plea and perhaps identifying with him as a fellow doctor, the medical department arranged for him to be housed in the prison infirmary—a much less threatening environment. Furthermore, the medical staff attempted to assist him in raising bail by calling bondsmen and trying to contact his family in the neighboring state.

Many parts of his story were rather suspicious; finally some staff members checked into it and found that he was not, as he alleged, with Air America, flying secret missions for the CIA in Vietnam, but was instead an unemployed laborer and college dropout from a reasonably affluent family in a neighboring state. Indeed, when his mother was finally contacted, she claimed that it was "good riddance" that he be in jail, that it was about time somebody caught up with him, and that neither she nor his stepfather were going to take any responsibility for him.

He became increasingly depressed and disoriented, and psychiatric evaluation indicated that he was a borderline schizophrenic. He was then returned to the prison population and received no psychiatric followup.

Shakespeare

Nineteen-year-old Shakespeare was awaiting trial on a homicide charge. He had a long history of incarceration in juvenile homes and since his seventeenth year he had passed two of his birthdays in jail.

Medical care was his major complaint. Not only was he concerned about his own medical care but the care of other inmates. He spent a large portion of his time arguing about the availability and quality of care with the medical staff. Specifically, he wanted to insure that both he and his friends had an adequate supply of drugs. Whenever the supply was cut off or threatened to be cut off, Shakespeare reverted to the threat: "I'm gonna cut up."

Indeed, he did cut up. One day he was carried into the medical department with fifty razor cuts, bleeding profusely—it took three hundred stitches to put Shakespeare back together again. Another time Shakespeare injected sputum into his foot. Why was he doing this? "To get the fuck out of this shit-eating prison."

He did get out, but when he came back the other inmates gave him a new nickname: Peg-leg.

Flash

They call him Flash—he was fifty-five, Black, and slow. He was in jail on an assault charge stemming from a fight that he had had with a neighbor.

Flash claimed to be a diabetic when he came in, but nobody believed him until the day he went into a diabetic coma. He died two days later in the hospital. It was also discovered that Flash was mentally retarded—perhaps the reason that he wasn't able to convince anyone of his medical history.

Correctional Officers

Bob
Sam
Ralph
Warden Oakes
Deputy Warden Brown
Assistant Deputy Warden Glasser

Bob

Three years ago Bob left a civil service job as a postman to become
a correctional officer. He had actually wanted to become a
policeman but was unable to pass the civil service examination.
His major reason for being in corrections was the security of the
job and the ability to be a member of the uniformed services of the
city.

His attitude toward inmates was certainly not negative, and indeed, at times, positive. He felt that he took his charge as a correctional officer seriously; he didn't think of himself as a jailer or as
the keeper of the keys. Generally, he felt that his job was not
particularly challenging and not particularly interesting. He liked
talking to the inmates and felt he was trying to help them as much
as possible.

However, he also felt that sometimes inmates took his helping
attitude as a sign of weakness and then they attempted to exploit
him—for example, inmates tried to get him to mail letters on the
outside or to pick up packages from their families. He thought that
many of the older correctional officers were lazy and stupid, and he
felt that his own correctional supervisors were not much better.

Sam

Sam, like all correctional officers, would pass through the entrance area in the morning and check his .38-caliber pistol. These pistols, interestingly enough, were only worn when correctional officers were off duty and were never worn inside the jail.

Sam was five feet ten inches tall and weighted close to 300 pounds. He was neither muscular nor neat. He related well to inmates and attempted to be friendly with them. Indeed, many inmates considered Sam to be one of the nicest correctional officers around. Perhaps this had something to do with his job, which was that of dispensing drugs to the inmates three times a day.

Sam worked hard but not on the job. In fact, his other job was as a truck driver, and he worked at that after and between shifts at the prison. After nine years on the job, it was learned that Sam was not only dispensing drugs that had been ordered but dispensing extra drugs for an additional income. He was brought up on departmental charges and fired, but not jailed.

Ralph

Ralph considered himself to be one of the sharpest correctional officers in the system. Physically he was tall, dark, well-dressed, and clean-cut.

He also considered himself to be an excellent judge of character. Based on this belief in himself and on his ability to communicate that belief to others, he was able to get the job of processing officer, which meant that he was in charge of assigning the inmates to the different work details that kept an inmate busy during the major part of a work shift.

It was not a particularly desired job, and Ralph made it into his personal empire. Ralph's only problem was that he wanted all the inmates to "respect him." Respect in Ralph's terms meant total obedience and total subservience. Inmates who disagreed with their job assignments or argued with Ralph were certain both to see the officious side of his character and to be assigned to the worst jobs.

During one prison uprising, word filtered through the prison that Ralph should be killed. Fortunately (for Ralph) he was on vacation.

Warden Oakes

Warden Oakes was an elected public official. The job of warden was a remnant of an earlier age of political patronage.

Years before, the warden did not need to go through the civil service to hire prison guards, correctional officers, clerks, and secretaries. And, therefore, being warden meant control of several hundred jobs. It was a much sought-after position and it was a position that involved little day-to-day operational responsibility for the prison.

However, political reform changed the patronage system, and very few of the jobs left in the prison are non-competitive. Nevertheless, the warden's job is considered an important political job because of its visibility; it is also considered a stepping stone to more important political positions such as mayor or congressman.

Warden Oakes is a graduate of a distinguished law school and very active in the correctional association's affairs. He talks glibly and sometimes extremely insightfully about prison problems. However, there is one difficulty: he never goes inside his own prison. He has been nicknamed ''The Phantom of the Prison.''

Deputy Warden Brown

Deputy Warden Brown is responsible for the operation of the prison. Small in stature, a "self-made man" who is a graduate of a local college and a correspondence-school legal studies program, he is not particularly liked by the prisoners and the staff because he is seen as the "guy who makes and enforces the rules."

The fact is, however, that while he is not particularly liked, he commands everyone's respect. The deputy warden is one of the few prison employees, including correctional officers, who dares to walk on the cellblocks without an armed escort. He has been known to walk into cellblocks and confront angry inmates eyeball-to-eyeball.

His honesty and integrity are beyond question, and this perhaps explains why he has an entree and rapport with the prisoners that no one else in the institution can claim. For example, he will periodically walk onto a cellblock and say, "Let me have all your weapons," and the inmates will in fact turn over their knives and guns to him without argument.

In turn, if an inmate complains to him, he can be sure that the complaint will be listened to and, if action is appropriate, the deputy will indeed act. His word is his bond; the inmates respect it and respect him because of it.

Assistant Deputy Warden Glasser

Assistant Deputy Warden Glasser has been in the correctional services for 22 years. During this time he has attended college at night and eventually won a Bachelor of Science degree in criminology.

He considers himself to be smarter than most correctional officers and prison administrators. His primary reason for being in the prison service is to earn enough money to retire at the age of 55 and, because of his status as a deputy assistant warden, he is able to develop a work schedule that permits him to hold a second job.

He has sent two children to college and built a sizable income from stocks and bonds. While not particularly fond of correctional work, he does like certain legal aspects and he is considered by many to be the jail-house lawyer. He invariably enters into debates with inmates over technical legal points, and when he appears about to lose a debate he "pulls rank" and points out to the inmate that he just doesn't know what he is talking about.

The assistant deputy warden has in a sense responded to what he describes as a "rather boring job" by developing special functional hobbies such as law.

Medical Staff

Dr. Nelson
Dr. Baker
Dr. Singer
Nurse Vogel
Nurse Griffin

Dr. Nelson

Dr. Nelson has been prison physician for 25 years. When he took the job initially it was his major responsibility. However, after about nine years of service he began spending less time at the prison and progressively more time developing what has become a sizable private practice.

He finds that inmates are generally uninteresting patients and that they tend to be a "pain in the ass." Although he is an internist, he has expressed interest in psychiatry and finds talking to patients much more rewarding than examining patients or studying their lab results.

He has many complaints about the prison health system such as lack of equipment, lack of space, and lack of assistance. He feels that all these things prevent him from doing a decent job. In general, he thinks that the care the inmates get in prison is about as good as they would get in his private practice. However, he just doesn't have the time because of the continuous demand to see him, as well as the countless emergencies that he senses are always coming up.

Dr. Baker

Dr. Baker a physician who is a recent graduate of medical school, has been working in a prison health system for about one year.

He feels that health care to inmates is unsatisfactory and that there is a need for revamping the system.

He is much distressed about his own practice of medicine with the inmates, having noticed that in the last year he has become considerably harder toward them, and that consequently the quality of his physical examinations has somehow decreased. He is really not sure about whether he will stay in prison health care—"It's just too damn debilitating."

Dr. Singer

Dr. Singer is a dentist who works part time in the prison and has worked there for the last five years. "It's a good source of regular income" but "It is difficult." "I usually don't get threatened by patients in my private practice and I am not really sure I want to stay with this." He finds that the work is basically that of extractions since inmates come in with "lousy, dirty mouths."

The most interesting work, which could perhaps restore the teeth, is not undertaken because of the lack of cooperation of inmates and the need for certain special services. For example, he notes that if one were to do certain restoration work on inmates they would have to go on special diets, which are just not available in the prison.

Nurse Vogel

For seven years Nurse Vogel has been the senior nurse in the prison medical department. She is extremely vocal and very unhappy with the entire prison medical system. She finds that she doesn't receive support from the warden and the deputies, and she finds the inmates neither respectful nor cooperative.

The doctor, she thinks, is great. In her opinion, he works under highly adverse conditions and he should be additionally rewarded. She has been vociferous about the need for more security and safety in her position. She approaches each inmate with a sense of superiority and fear—fear of being raped or of being beaten up. This fear is translated into rather terse, formal, and nonhelpful medical behavior toward the inmates.

Nurse Griffin

Nurse Griffin is 27 years old and has just started work in the prison health system.

For the last five years she was senior staff nurse in a local hospital. She came to work in the prison because of the regular working hours. She finds her work, which is that of checking physician perscriptions and handing out medication, to be extremely boring and totally uninteresting. The inmates she finds to be fairly reasonable, and she has not had any problems.

She is not particularly fearful, and she finds that her rapport with the Black inmates (she is Black) is quite good. Her initial disturbance about being in a prison and seeing "so many guys who say, and I believe them, that they are up on bum raps. But, after a week of not sleeping I started ignoring them, and now I'm OK."

Part 4

Directions

CHAPTER 8

Directions for the Future

A snapshot of prison health care in the United States is not a pleasant picture. In general, on the four scales by which health care is traditionally measured—accessibility, quality, continuity, and efficiency—prisons and jails receive an unsatisfactory rating.

More specifically, accessibility implies the availability of a reasonable quantity of comprehensive services. Prisons generally do not meet these requirements. For example, almost half of the jails in the United States have no adequate medical facilities. Is it not reasonable to expect that, in any location where there is a large aggregation of human beings, medical care should be available? What is really needed to provide these services?

Financial support is certainly one element. However, the element of greatest importance is a commitment by the general and professional community to the basic concept that any person, regardless of his particular social status at a particular instant in time, is entitled to medical care.

Assuming care is available, then how can a system be so arranged as to insure that those needing care can get to that care? Clearly, enough is now known about the organization of prisons and prisoners to arrange a system that guarantees personal accessibility. Using hallboys, as was done in the case of New Orleans, is a certain way of minimizing accessibility to the system.

A last consideration under accessibility is comprehensive care. The system must be so organized as to minimize needless human and fiscal expenditures and utilize all information and resources to the maximum. A good example of how not to do it was the New York City case, where inmates may have two or three physicals per year but each entrance into prison is treated as a totally discrete event, having no relationship to the admission preceding it or to the admission that may occur in three months.

Quality requires having at the outset the right number of professional and non-professional employees available for provision of the services. Furthermore, it requires physicians with the appropriate level of skill. In this age of specialization, a physician is not simply a physician. If a prison needs a general medical officer, it is imperative that an internist or a general practitioner be hired. But to use pediatric or opthalmic residents simply because they are available is to handicap the system immediately.

Continuity implies that services are person-centered and coordinated. Coordination in a prison is not a difficult task simply because a prison is a fairly closed system. Person-centered service is a function of the professionals recruited into the system and the seriousness of the task that they see. They, as well as the others responsible for the prison, must recognize the importance of medical care if the system is to function well.

Efficiency, the final element in medical care, involves sound administration of the program. Obviously in prison and out of prison there is a scarcity of resources. A good system conserves resources so that they can be used as hedges against future scarcities.

For example, prison health systems, by practicing preventive medicine, can in fact build the health of their penal community and thereby economize in the long run. Unfortunately, few prison health systems approach their patients with such an attitude.

The prognosis, with few exceptions, is grim—can a prescription for the future be offered?

Yes! There are at least two courses of action that offer considerable promise.

First, there is the idea of "contracting-out" for services. This approach (as described in the New Orleans case) requires that the jail or prison contract for medical services with another organization, such as a hospital, medical school, or group practice, which has expertise in delivering medical care.

Second, this approach requires that both the prison administration and the organization providing the care enter into a carefully conceived written agreement that clearly delineates the elements of medical care to be provided in the prison. The third important facet of this approach is that an independent group (such as the local health department or outside consultants) should monitor the quality of care. Such an arrangement results in medical care being provided and monitored by professionals under the administrative direction of those with the ultimate responsibility for the inmates.

A second approach is that of reorganizing an existing medical department. This process should begin with the delineation of the department objectives. Input for this first step should come from inmates, correctional officers, the prison administration, and, most important, the entire staff of the medical department. Next, the medical department must develop programs to meet those objectives, and, finally, after assessing its resources, the department must assign to various individuals authority and responsibility for using the resources to attain the objectives.

Both of the aforementioned proposals require the rational allocation of health care resources. Obviously, variations on the themes of "contracting-out" and "reorganization," as well as other approaches, can be developed. Moreover, the use of one approach should never preclude change to a different mode of delivering care. Indeed, what may work at a particular time in the history of an organization may not work at another time—hence the need for continual evaluation.

Finally, the problem of health care in jails and prisons can be and has been ignored for many decades. Intellectual as well as total financial resources are now in greater abundance than at any time in the history of man—failure to solve this problem is indeed a reproach to mankind.

Appendices

APPENDIX A

The Status of Health Status Indicators

Throughout this volume considerable attention has been given to the problems of decision making in prison health services. These problems are, to a major extent, related to the more generic issue of decision making in the voluntary and public sectors of the economy where the definition of satisfactory outcomes is somewhat vague.

Several years ago, in an attempt to bring some order out of an admittedly controversial and chaotic situation, the author prepared the following paper for the Association of State and Territorial Health Officers, under a contract from the Health Services and Mental Health Administration and originally published in Health Services Report *(87:3, March, 1972, pages 212–220) under the title of "The Status of Health Status Indicators."*

This paper should be of value to those whose primary interest is improvement of the effectiveness of the system that delivers health care to prison inmates.

Physicians and other professionals are continually called upon to make decisions about treatment and programs intended to affect the health of individuals and populations. This enormous responsibility makes understanding the measures of health imperative. Toward this end, a review of the status of health status indicators was undertaken. Specifically addressed were the following questions: What is health? What are the purposes of health status indicators? What are the problems in developing adequate measures of health? What is the present state of the art in measuring health status? Are any of the new and developing health status indicators practical? And finally, what is the outlook for health status indicators?

The Concept of Health

The most often quoted definition of health is that of the World Health Organization: "Health is a state of complete physical, mental, and social well-being, and not merely the absence of diseases and infirmity."[1] Widely criticized for its abstractness and simplicity, the WHO definition is nevertheless useful in an uncritical environment or in those instances when the public is unwilling to ask, ''What techniques do you have to produce physical, mental, and social well-being in those who are free from disease or infirmity?''[2]

Sigerist offered a similar definition of health: ''Health is, therefore, not simply the absence of disease: it is something positive, a joyful attitude toward life, and a cheerful acceptance of the responsibilities that life puts on the individual.''[3] Another definition and idea offered by Sigerist was that of health as an undisturbed rhythm, ''We all live in a specific rhythm, determined by nature, culture, and habit. Day and night alternate in an unending ebb and flow, and we ourselves conform to this rhythm with waking and sleeping, with work and rest. . . . An undisturbed rhythm means health. . . . Disease then strikes abruptly into this structure.''[4]

Others also have offered definitions: Wylie's modification of Spencer's definition, ''Health is the perfect, continuing adjustment of an organism to its environment. Conversely, disease would be an imperfect continuing adjustment'';[5] Hoyman's definition, ''Health is optimal personal fitness for full, fruitful, creative living'';[6] Lifson's definition, ''Health is the degree to which a human's functions (sensing, data processing, motioning . . .) are performed and pain is absent'';[7] Romano's definition, ''Health consists in the capacity of the organism to maintain a balance in which it may be reasonably free of undue pain, discomfort, disability or limitation of action including social capacity'';[8] and finally, Blum's modification of Romano's definition, ''Health consists of: (1) the capacity of the organism to maintain a balance appropriate to its age and social needs in which it is reasonably free of gross dissatisfaction, discomfort, disease, or disability; and (2) to behave in ways which promote the survival of the species as well as the self-fulfillment or enjoyment of the individual.''[9]

The problems with these definitions are ambiguity and abstruseness. For example, how does one translate into operational language concepts such as ''social well-being,'' ''cheerful acceptance,'' ''rhythm,'' ''continuing adjustment,'' ''fruitful-creative living,'' ''balance appropriate,'' or ''gross dissatisfaction''? Where in these definitions is the relationship between disease, environment, and health taken into account? Finally, where in these definitions is the perspective of the definer recognized? Individual persons, practicing physicians, public health officials, families, and society view health differently. To an individual person, good health may be "feeling well" or absence of discomfort; to a physician, it might be absence of clinical disease, and, perhaps to society, health is closely associated with the individual's fulfilling his social role.

These definitional difficulties should not be considered lightly. Just as the iinability to clearly define the objectives of any program or organization leads to the operational difficulty of measuring advancement toward a diffuse goal, so our inability to define health leads to the obvious problems of not being able to measure health status. This difficulty of conceptualizing health is perhaps the major constraint on the development and usefulness of health status indicators. Nevertheless, this constraint is tempered to a degree by the purposes and functions that health status indicators are meant to serve.

Purposes of Health Status Indicators

But what are these purposes? Wilbur Cohen, while Secretary of the Department of Health, Education, and Welfare, suggested that indicators help keep score, that is, they can tell the status of the nation's health as well as the progress that is being made toward its betterment.[10] At the most basic level he is no doubt correct.

A somewhat more comprehensive idea, however, is presented by Bickner.[11] He suggests that health status indicators serve three primary functions: public information, administration, and medical science. The first function is simply that of giving readily understandable information, in the form of a consumer price index of health, to the public. This information would be used by health professionals as a means of informing the general public and the legislatures on the health situation in order to gain more attention for health. In operational terms, this means that the indices would give the public and the legislatures the readily understandable and digestible information they need to allocate more money for health.

The second function, Bickner suggests, is administration. Here he notes that indices of health status would help managers be better health planners, evaluators, financial managers, and administrative decision makers. Medical science, the third function for health status indicators, would help those who are interested in performing descriptive and experimental research in medical care. In summary, Bickner offers the crucial concept that a health status indicator must be considered from the perspective of the dynamic need that the indicator fulfills.

Defining health and clarifying the purposes of health status indicators, then, are two major problems encountered in developing an index of health. Other problems are validity, reliability, data sources, and cost.

Problems

Validity of measurement means that what is actually being measured is what is purportedly being measured. For example, the National Health Survey uses interview reports to determine disability data; and, as Sullivan points out, the validity of these data "is difficult to evaluate because there is often no criterion for comparison."[12] Furthermore, he notes that "the validity of disability data based on interview reports will be open to question until extensive use of such measures in a variety of studies has established their relation to clinical measures on the one hand and social variables on the other."[13] In one attempt to test the validity of interview data in relation to clinical data, Meltzer and Hochstim encountered several methodological problems but still found what appeared to be a low validity level.[14]

Reliability of measurement is a concern with the accuracy of the measuring instrument; that is, does the instrument consistently give the same reading when measuring the same phenomenon. Sullivan's statement on this issue is most significant:

> Reliable measurement requires elimination or control of extraneous factors influencing the measurement. Since a primary purpose of a health index is comparison over time, evaluation of reliability should take into consideration both factors influencing measurement under current circumstances and the possibility of measurements over time being distorted by irrelevant social changes. Methodological studies have shown that many aspects of survey procedure influence the measures obtained.[15]

Data sources and cost are perhaps the major fixed constraints on developing indices of health. If it were agreed that disability or productive man-years were appropriate indices of health, how would data be obtained? Special surveys could be designed or secondary sources of data, such as absentee records of schools and plants, might be used. However, if one wanted to refine these data for reliability and validity, problems of nonavailability and cost of information would be encountered.

This last point, cost, is an obvious restriction about which little is said or written. But, for example, if one wanted to replicate the National Health Interview Survey sample in the state of California it would cost between $1.2 and $2.4 million, while the Office of Economic Opportunity estimates a cost of from $30 to $80 per household interview (this includes basic data processing). How many states, cities, or other political subdivisions could afford to spend a comparable amount of money to get questionably valid data about poorly defined concepts for often incomprehensible purposes?

Presently Utilized Indicators

Regardless of the problems in developing adequate measures of health, many indicators are being used and a number of new indicators have been proposed. Mortality and morbidity have been the traditional measures of health. Death is the well-defined and recorded event that has had great value as an indicator until very recently.

In a discussion of this situation, Moriyama states: "The past declines in the death rate at the various ages are due primarily to reductions in the death rate for infectious diseases . . . by 1950 the mortality from the diseases of infectious origins had reached a level where death rates for the infectious diseases no longer contributed in a major way to the overall mortality rate . . . Further reductions in total mortality in the United States are possible, but any substantial decreases must come from the lowering of the death rates for chronic noninfective diseases and for accidents and other violence."[16] Moriyama concludes that, "The nature of the past changes in mortality and the past behavior of the death rates have made moot the value of statistics of deaths from all causes as a measure of health in countries like the U.S."

Infant mortality is, perhaps, the most popular of the mortality indices. Widely quoted, the figure has been most often used to compare the level of health of the United States and other countries. Typically, a public official notes that the U.S. infant mortality rate is higher than 12 to 15 other countries. To him, this means we are not doing a very good job with health. While the reliability of infant mortality data is still in question, it nevertheless has been demonstrated that this statistic "appears to no longer [be] a particularly useful indicator of the level of living and sanitary conditions for a country like the United States."[17] Nevertheless, after all the arguments are evaluated, mortality is the only identifiable common denominator of health status and, thus, its value should not be categorically dismissed.

Morbidity is conceptually and pragmatically more difficult to use as a health status indicator than mortality. Conceptually, one encounters the problems of definition and classification. When is a person sick? How sick is sick? How should different morbid states be classified—very morbid, medium morbid, and not so morbid? Pragmatically, there are problems with cost, reliability, and validity. How can the different morbid states be measured? How can assurances be built into the system so that a measurement taken by one person on one day is comparable to another's measurement on a different day? A classic example of the problems encountered in some morbidity studies is discussed by Zola, who found that levels and types of complaints varied among different ethnic groups for the same apparent clinically evidenced disease.[18] Obviously, morbidity does not equal morbidity.

The National Health Survey makes extensive use of a variety of morbidity indicators. Reports generated by this research present data on the populations' acute and chronic conditions, days lost from work and school, activity limitations by degree—major, some, and none—hospital days, numbers of physician and dentist visits, and the interval since last physician visit. While great care is taken in training interviewers and establishing definitions for this extremely sophisticated study, the national survey, as Sullivan noted,[19] still encounters problems in reliability of measurements. For example, in a special study of hospitalization it was found that there was underreporting based on the disease, the patient and family's socioeconomic status, the length of stay in the hospital, the elapsed time since the hospitalization, and the relationship of the reporter to the patient.[20]

The health examination portion of the National Health Survey was confounded by seasonal and geographic measurement variances, cost of training examiners, and quality control of the laboratory work. Perhaps more significant is the limited extent of the medical examination; that is, in the adult physical, the physicians' appraisal of the patient included neither an abdominal nor an internal examination. In discussing the value of the Health Examination Survey, the designers suggest that, "the results will be the product of highly standardized measurements on a probability sample of the population and that these measurements were selected initially because a good many qualified people thought them relevant to a wide variety of purposes."[21]

A final, traditional indicator of health status worth noting because of its popularity might be classified generically as an activity count. The rationale for using these counts as indicators is the assumption that the number of services provided and personnel and facilities available are related to health status. This assumption leads one to conclude that the health status of a community is higher if it has a higher physician-population ratio than another community. Is this valid? Perhaps citizens from east Baltimore or parts of Boston would not reach the offered conclusion.

Activity counts require considerable refinement and probably a greater focus on smaller subsegments of the population before they will be sufficiently sensitive indicators. But, even if that were possible, it must be remembered that activity counts are only quantitative indicators—and, as such, do not account for the qualitative aspects of medical care. Examples of activity counts used as indicators of health status are easily found.

The following general medical care indicators are listed in a 1969 Department of Health, Education, and Welfare document:[22]

● Non-federal hospital beds and utilization rates, by type of hospital, United States, 1950–1967

● Annual physician visits per person, by age and sex, United States, 1964–1967

● Annual disability days per person by family income, type of disability, and age, July 1966 to July 1967

● Non-federal physicians, by region and major professional activity, December 1967

● Registered nurses by field of employment and educational preparation, United States, January 1967

• Registered nurses employed for public health work, by type of agency, United States, 1966 and 1968
• Physician availability, by region and major professional activity, December 1967
• Registered and practical nurses in practice, estimated number and rate per 100,000 population, United States 1950–1968.

The Office of Economic Opportunity's surveys of health centers use a combination of activity counts and morbidity type data.[23] Their varied list of health indicators comprises activity limitation caused by chronic conditions, bed disability days, usual source of care, interval since last physician visit, total physician visits, hospital admissions, length of stay, post-hospital physician visits, dental visits, and dental care received.

A combination of activity indicators and morbidity data were used as health indicators in the Census Use Study. Deshaies reports, for example, that the following health status indicators were used: prematurity, prenatal care utilization, outpatient clinic utilization, physician and dentist utilization, degree of disability in the population, and prevalence of morbidity in the population.[24]

Evaluation Criteria for Indicators

The preceding criticisms indicate a need for criteria for evaluation of health status indicators, a subject which both Sullivan and Moriyama have considered. Sullivan suggests two primary criteria for an index of health: (a) it should show changes over time in significant aspects of the health of the living as well as in mortality and (b) it should be subject to analysis into components which provide a useful description of health problems underlying index values.[25]

Moriyama states that an index of health should have certain desirable properties, such as (a) it should be meaningful and understandable, (b) it should be sensitive to variation in the phenomenon being measured, (c) the assumption underlying the index should be theoretically justifiable and intuitively reasonable, (d) it should consist of clearly defined components, (e) each component should make an independent contribution to variations in the phenomenon being measured, and (f) the index should be derivable from data that are quite feasible to obtain.[26]

Bush and Fanshel's suggestions on criteria are also insightful. They state:

> To be widely accepted and used, a quantitative output indicator must integrate morbidity with mortality data, and allow comparisons across disease categories and agency lines. It must be acceptable in a pluralistic health system, where the elements are only loosely coupled together, and agreement among multiple decisionmakers about common goals is difficult. It must serve as a guide to data collection, since much expensive data gathering is unrelated to the goals of the system and contributes little to real decisions. Finally, the end-product or output of the health system must be defined clearly enough that it can be related to a wide range of resource inputs and activity indicators, allowing performance analyses of various health programs.[27]

Finally, the following are my criteria for health status indices, some of which are partly borrowed from Sullivan and Moriyama:
• The purpose of the health status indicator should be clearly stated. For example, is the health status indicator meant to be used for public information purposes, program priorities, or what?
• The numerator and denominator data used to compute the index should be readily understandable not only by those who will use the indices, for example, planners, but by those who will supposedly be influenced by the index, for example, legislators.
• The data used for computation must be presently available from existing data sources with minimal modifications.
• The process of computing the data must be readily understood by those who will be using the data.
• The components of the index must be clearly identifiable and their individual effects on the total index must be distinguishable.
• The data used in the index must be reliable and valid.
• There must be a built-in mechanism to evaluate the validity of the measure by correlating measures of health status with other measures of social well-being.

These various criteria for evaluating indices of health should be kept in mind as a number of new and developing health status indicators are reviewed. Older works, such as those by Sanders[28] and Fanshel and Bush,[29] have been reviewed elsewhere and are not discussed here.

State of the Art

Sullivan[30] recently proposed a general index of health that would combine mortality and morbidity data and would be sensitive to changes in health status over time. The mortality data would be provided through presently available life expectancy tables, and the morbidity part of the index would use information from the National Health Survey. As a general index at the national level, Sullivan's idea is probably operational although, as he notes, data can be obtained only for the total population and a few major population categories. Perhaps the most significant limitation is that of not having enough appropriate data. This problem, Sullivan states, is, "likely to preclude application of the indices for States or local areas for the foreseeable future."[31]

Another operational health status index that is presently being tested is the Indian Health Service's Q index.[32] The purpose of this measure is to provide managers who are setting program priorities with quantitative information on the cost-benefit relationships of different programs. This indicator derives a Q value by using a fairly simple formula with two major components. One compontent is a ratio of the age- and sex-adjusted mortality experience of the Indian population and the total U.S. population arrived at by multiplying the crude mortality rate of the years lost because of premature death among Indians. The other major component is derived from the hospital days and outpatient visits of the Indian population.

The Q index basically uses activity counts—hospital days and outpatient visits—as a surrogate of morbidity; not included, however, is any measure of disability. In a discussion of the index, Miller notes that, "the Q value correlates closely with determinations based on professional judgments. In at least one instance when the value was used on an experimental basis in a slightly different form than described here, the index was judged applicable and beneficial in an urban setting."[33]

The value of Q as an index for setting program priority should be seriously considered since, even with its shortcomings, it is readily computed, it is understandable, and it can work with presently available data although linkage of the data may be both cumbersome and costly.

The Northeast Ohio Regional Medial Program has postulated a general health status index. The basic formula states that the health of the population is a function of genetic and socioeconomic factors and "the application of health services to manifest need."[34] The operability of this notion is based on some debatable premises. For example, it was assumed that "for diseases with a high risk of death, such as heart disease, cancer, and stroke, morbidity parallels mortality and that mortality data alone could be substituted for morbidity and mortality data."[35] With this substitution, the final formula offered was not for the health of the general population but rather the health status of the population with heart disease, cancer, and stroke. Another problem with this formulation is that somewhere between the initial conceptualization and final verbalization the formula is rewritten to account for the fixed constraints of available data, thus leaving the following equation:

$$\left(\frac{1}{\text{age adjusted death rate}} \right) = f \left(\frac{\text{crude discharge statistics}}{\text{crude area deaths}} \right) \left(\begin{array}{c} \text{genetic and} \\ \text{socioeconomic} \\ \text{factors} \end{array} \right) \left(\frac{\text{other medical services}}{\text{deaths}} \right)$$

A final and obvious criticism relates to the absence of any quantitative measures of the genetic and socioeconomic factors. Since these are components of all the equations, and are, obviously, of some importance, how shall they be treated? The formula, while conceptually interesting, appears to be neither operational nor practical. With careful development, however, the formula might provide a meaningful, relevant, and needed general index of health.

An index that demonstrates many of the problems with health status indicators was developed by the Human Population Laboratory of the California State Health Department in Berkeley. Basically, three dimensions of health are considered—physical health, mental health, and social health, Estimations of these dimensions are arrived at by means of a 23-page self-administered questionnaire.

For physical health, questions are asked about "33 specific complaints—five types of functional disability, 14 chronic conditions, three impairments, and 11 symptoms associated with chronic illness.''[36] The mental health spectrum is a measure of psychological well-being based on answers to a number of questions in the questionnaire. The third part of the health spectrum considered is that of social health, an index comprised of four dimensions—marital relationship, employability, community involvement, and social integration. To date, testing of reliability and validity of the physical health spectrum indicates that the survey of physical health has high reliability but questionable validity. The instrument, then, does an excellent job of measuring what it measures, but what it measures is in doubt.

The problem of measuring something, assuming it is health and, therefore, calling it health, is not unusual with health status indicators. Yet, when other independent measures of health are considered vis-a-vis health status indicators, the first-measure correlations are not consistently high. Consistently high correlations between classes of indicators should be required before indicators are accepted for use. Methods for testing are necessary; and, toward this end, the Human Population Laboratory's work is a significant step forward.

Indices of health have also been derived through the use of mathematical models. Chiang, for example, developed a health index by combining a measure of the frequency of illness, the duration of illness, and finally, mortality. Several problems exist with regard to Chiang's work. First, the data for the final health index formula are provided by a variety of poorly understood formulas. Second, the data for inclusion in the formulas, while perhaps available nationally, may not be available on a state or local level. Finally, as a concept, the answer to the question, "What is the average fraction of the year in which an individual is healthy?"[37] that is, finding the "mean duration of health" is not an appropriate index of a population's health. Again, this conceptual formulation accounts for but one aspect of health, that is, the quantity of life, with no regard to the qualitative and nonphysical dimensions of health.

Other mathematically oriented procedures, such as factor analysis, have been used to derive health indices. Lawton and associates, for example, looked at 30 different indices of health in an attempt to find a common structure, or several common structures, among the indices. Their final list of health factors is definitionally vague and not impressive when one realizes that the factor loadings and explained variances are low, particularly since they used 30

items and ten rotations. Their conclusions, however, are significant: "The factor structure of indices of health is quite complex
. . . and . . . We hope that this study and others . . . will put to rest
the idea that there is a single concept of health which may eventually be reduced to an operational definition."[38]

The risk profile is an operations research approach presently
being tied at the Mount Sinai Medical School. This model uses pre-
existing data to generate a risk profile for each patient under its
care. From this model, one could hypothesize that as the risks for
an individual or community lessened, its state of health had improved. Still in the developmental stage, this idea appears promis-
ing, although it seemingly requires massive amounts of existing and
new data as well as much judgmental input from health professionals.

Mathematical models are also being developed in the health index project of Bush and Fanshel.[39] In this project, heath status is
divided into a number of different functional levels, ranging from
well-being to death. Probabilities for movements from one level to
another based on different programmatic situations are devised by
professional value judgments. The mathematics of the process as
well as the sources of data are sometimes obscure, but the project's
work does raise hope for the development of a workable index. The
major limitation of this work is noted by the researchers: "all such
applications [mathematical] hinge on methods to empirically define the states and determine their values."[40]

A final category of indices might be called proxy measures.
In 1969 Kisch and associates[41] proposed a proxy measure that
would consist of four questions dealing with days of hospitalization, drug usage, acute conditions, and chronic conditions. The
validity of the questionnaire, self-administered by patients, was
tested on two occasions by having two physicians, based on the
records of medical history and physical examination, rate each
patient as being in good health, medium health, or poor health.

On both pretests, a high degree of agreement was found
between the proxy score generated by the self-administered questionnaire and the physicians' ratings, although the proxy score
overestimated the number of patients in good health. Limitations
offered by the authors are, "that the proxy measure is a survey
research tool . . . not suitable for physical examination or medical
history [and that it] is a significant but, nonetheless, biased pre-
dictor of patient health."[42]

Other criticisms of this proxy measure are the assumption that the physicians' judgment, based on an examination of records, is the appropriate indicator of health status; the use of only two physicians as raters—perhaps five physicians' ratings would be more valid; and finally, the insensitivity of the good, medium, and poor health categorization. Essentially, the proxy measure is not dissimilar to a self-administered medical history and the standard of good to poor health is a generally agreed upon value judgment of the professionals.

Perhaps at the other extreme of proxy measures is the use of economic attributes as indirect measures of health status. Such attributes could be income, employment, demographic, or residence measures. In some studies these economic indices have been correlated with various mortality rates and morbidity rates. The correlations tend to be high; but are the correlating health statistics appropriate measures of health status? For example, if a particular economic index is closely correlated with mortality, the correlation does not legitimize either the mortality data or the economic data as health status indicators.

In summary, much work is underway in the development of health status indicators. Field tests are being planned or are in operation for Sullivan's new general index of health and Miller's Q index. The California Health Department's goal is to devise a "method of indexing health status that can be used to monitor the condition of the population and in turn alert the State to developing problems."[43] The Office of Economic Opportunity has collected a large amount of data, and, with Systems Sciences, it is working toward development of more sophisticated general health indicators. The risk profile concept in use at Mount Sinai Medical School may also turn out to be a feasible health status indicator. Finally, Bush and Fanshel's research may result in a workable index of health.

Unfortunately, all the projects mentioned have two common problems—conceptualization and value judgments. The problem of conceptualization cannot be ignored. What is health? A clear (or clearer) conceptualization of health is needed before significant progress can be made in measuring health. It is hoped that Prof. Monroe Lerner's interest and research at Johns Hopkins University in the conceptualization of health will make major contributions toward a framework in which health can be understood. In addition, it is expected that Dr. Sidney Katz of the Michigan

Department of Public Health will continue with his work directed toward finding and tying together the common thread presented in health status indicators over the years. This too will make a tremendous contribution toward the development of health status indicators.

The problem of value judgments is perhaps the least discussed. Realistically, since value judgments enter into health status indicators, one must ask how these judgments should be made. Should they be made in the traditional blind manner or should appropriately sophisticated methods be utilized or developed? Discussions and reports of scrtuiny of the process and methods for making value judgments have recently entered the literature. For example, in late 1970 Fanshel and Bush[44] expressed concern about methods and used the paired comparison method for making judgments about assignment of different weights to states of function and dysfunction. Another, certainly simpler, method was used in Wisconsin where a questionnaire, containing many health status indicators, was sent by the Wisconsin Department of Health and Social Services during the summer of 1970 to a number of health professionals for their opinion on the planning value of each of the indicators.

At present, no method or concept for making value judgments is flawless. Therefore, it must be concluded that research is necessary to find the most reasonable ways for both the public and the professionals to make their value judgments.

Conclusion

Those who are searching for valid indicators of health status should recognize first the limitations of this particular review; that is, it is concerned only with general health status indicators. Environmental health indicators, for example, although somewhat related to general health status indicators, were not included in this report. Second, all but the grossest indicator, mortality, require some degree of value judgment; present methods for making these judgments are poorly understood and demand considerable study. Next, physicians and other health professionals should recognize the conceptual problems in developing health status indicators—the administrative strategy of muddling through has no place in dealing with the crucial matter of health. Finally, it should be recognized that the fixed constraints of data availability and cost put

realistic limitations on any new system of gathering input information for health status measures.

A recommendation for action could be adoption of one or
several presently existing (theoretical or experimental) indicators.
On the other hand, perhaps at present no action should be undertaken. The first recommendation is more attractive because of
its decisiveness and action orientation. Implied in such a decision
is faith in the reliability and validity of the selected indicators. This
faith must be strong because once a system is changed to collect
data for the indicator, it will be bound to that indicator. Of course,
parallel data-gathering efforts also could be set up that would not
affect the present system; this might be conceptually acceptable,
but it is pragmatically difficult to buy (or sell) on the basis of cost.

The recommendation of no action, perhaps less attractive
because of its lack of decisiveness, is predicated on two factors.
First, it regards presently existing indicators as generally unaccep-
table and, second, it implies a faith in future developments.

If one believes, as the author does, that researchers like Bush,
Fanshel, Katz, Lerner, Miller, Sullivan, and others are on the right
track toward conceptualizing health and developing indices to
measure it, then "swinging" with one indicator or group of indicators at the present time is inappropriate. However, if, judging
by the slow, unsteady, and insignificant progress toward finding
health status indicators, one believes that the future is unlikely to
herald major breakthroughs, then it might be appropriate to select
and use the best available indices.

This discussion has considered health status indicators from
both the conceptual and pragmatic viewpoints. The opinions and
ideas expressed are based on both a review of the literature and on
many discussions of the subject with scores of people throughout
the country to whom the author is grateful—and apologetic for any
possible misconceptions.

References

[1]World Health Organization: The first ten years of the World Health Organization.
WHO, Geneva, 1958, p. 459.

[2]Wylie, C. M.: The definition and measurement of health and disease. Public
Health Rep 85: 101–104, February 1970.

[3]Sigerist, H. E.: Medicine and human welfare. Yale University Press, New
Haven, 1941, p. 100.

[4]Sigerist, H. E.: On the sociology of medicine, edited by Milton I. Roemer. MD Publications, Inc. New York, 1960, pp. 10, 11,

[5]Wylie: *op. cit.*, p. 103.

[6]Hoyman, H. S.: Our modern concept of health. Paper presented at the American Public Health Association, annual meeting, Detroit, Mich. Nov. 16, 1961, p. 1.

[7]Lifson, M. W.: Definitions of terminology. List prepared for the California Center for Health Services Research. Los Angeles, May 1969. Mimeographed.

[8]Romano, J.: Basic orientation and education of the medical student. JAMA 143: 409–412. June 3, 1950.

[9]Blum, H. L.: A working definition of health for planners: Merging concepts. University of California School of Public Health, Berkeley, 1971, pp. 22, 23. Mimeographed.

[10]U.S. Department of Health, Education, and Welfare: Toward a social report. U.S. Government Printing Office, Washington, D.C., 1969, pp. xii, xiii.

[11]Bickner, R. E.: Measurement and indices of health. *In* Conference series. Outcomes conference I–II. Methodology of identifying, measuring and evaluating outcomes of health service programs, systems and subsystems. Health Services and Mental Health Administration, Rockville, Md. 1970, pp. 133–149.

[12]National Center for Health Statistics: Conceptual problems in developing an index of health. PHS Publication No. 1000, Ser. 2, No. 17. U.S. Government Printing Office, Washington, D.C., 1966.

[13]*Ibid.*: p. 15.

[14]Meltzer, J. W., and Hochstim, J. R.: Reliability and validity of survey data on physical health. Public Health Rep 85: 1075–1086, December 1970.

[15]National Center for Health Statistics: *op. cit.*, p. 14.

[16]Moriyama, I. M.: Problems in the measurement of health status, *In* Indicators of social change, edited by E. Sheldon and W. Moore. Russell Sage Foundation, New York, 1968, pp. 576, 577.

[17]*Ibid.*

[18]Zola, I.: Culture and symptoms: An analysis of patients' presenting complaints. Am Social Rev 31: 615–630, October 1966.

[19]National Center for Health Statistics: *op. cit.*, p. 14.

[20]National Center for Health Statistics: Reporting of hospitalization in the health interview survey. PHS Publication No. 1000, Ser. 2, No. 6. U.S. Government Printing Office, Washington, D.C., 1965.

[21]National Center for Health Statistics: Plan and initial program of the health examination survey. PHS Publication No. 1000, Ser. 1, No. 4. U.S. Government Printing Office, Washington, D.C., 1965, p. 19.

[22]U.S. Department of Health, Education, and Welfare: Congressional hearings data book, fiscal year 1970. Health Services and Mental Health Administration, Community Profile Data Center, Rockville, Md., 1969, p. 159.

[23]Banacki, J. R.: Franklin C. Fetter Family Health Center survey, Charleston, South Carolina. National Opinion Research Center, Chicago, 1970. pp. 16–45.

[24]Deshaies, J.: New Haven health information system. U.S. Census Bureau, Washington, D.C., Mar. 17, 1971. Mimeographed.

[25]National Center for Health Statistics: Conceptual problems in developing an index of health, p. 2.

[26]Moriyama: *op. cit.*, p. 593.

[27]Bush, J. W., and Fanshel, S.: Basic concepts for quantifying health status program outcomes, 1970. Health Index Project. Graduate School of Public Administration, New York University, Nov. 15, 1970. Mimeographed.

[28]Sanders B.S.: Measuring community health levels. Am J Public Health 54: 1063–1070, July 1964.

[29]Fanshel, S., and Bush, J. W.: A health status index and its application for health services outcomes. Operations Res 18: 1021–1066. November-December 1970.

[30]Sullivan, D. F.: A single index of mortality and morbidity. HSMHA Health Rep 86: 347–354, April 1971.

[31]*Ibid.*: p. 353.

[32]Miller, J. E.: An indicator to aid management in assigning program priorities. Public Health Rep 85: 725–731, August 1970.

[33]*Ibid.*: p. 730.

[34]Northeast Ohio Regional Medical Program: Part II. Health related data. Section IV. Hospital discharge study. Northeast Ohio Regional Medical Program, Cleveland, 1968, p. 25.

[35]*Ibid.*

[36]Meltzer and Hochstim: *op. cit.*, p. 1076.

[37]National Center for Health Statistics: An index of health: Mathematical models. PHS Publication No. 1000, Ser. 2, No. 5. U.S. Government Printing Office, Washington, D.C., 1965, p. 10.

[38]Lawton, M. P., Ward, M., and Yaffe, S.: Indices of health in an aging population. J. Gerontol 22: 334–342, July 1967.

[39]Bush and Fanshel: *op. cit.*, pp. 3,4.

[40]*Ibid.*, p. 60.

[41]Kisch, A. I., Kovner, J. W., Harris, L. J., and Kline, G.: New proxy measure for health status. Health Serv Res 4: 223–230, fall 1969.

[42]*Ibid.*, p. 230.

[43]California Department of Public Health: Indicators of physical health in California. Berkeley, December 1970. Mimeographed.

[44]Fanshel and Bush: *op. cit.*

APPENDIX B

Health and Medical Services

For several decades reasonable and attainable standards for health care services in prisons and jails have existed. The appendices which follow present two of the most commonly available sets of standards. Appendix B is excerpted from Chapter 26, pages 436—442, of Manual of Correctional Standards *(Washington, D.C.; American Correctional Association, 1966).*

Medical Care is essential for individual well being. The services provided in a health and medical care program should be of the highest standard. These services should be rendered under conditions satisfactory to both the recipients and the professions providing the services. The quality of a medical care program will depend upon the philosophy as well as the qualifications of those who render the services. A high standard of care requires both scientific and organizational elements incorporated into a plan which can be subjected to certain measurements for purposes of evaluation. The qualitative standards for medical care programs must be somewhat flexible to reflect the ever changing social and scientific patterns of the times. A health program for prisoners should be organized to permit experimentation and change in both its scientific and organizational content.

Objectives and Standards

The objectives of a health and medical services program for prisoners must include the promotion of health, the prevention of disease and disability, the cure or mitigation of disease, and the rehabilitation of the patient.

Good medical care cannot be promoted when services are rendered on the basis of a double standard, as for instance, one for "paying patients" and one for "public charges." To achieve the goals set down above, medical care programs for prisoners must be equivalent in quality to the care which is available in the community. Acceptance of a lesser standard will make impossible the achievement of these goals.

Dignity, freedom, and individuality must be maintained by those who provide as well as those who receive medical services. This goal is consistent with the service tradition of the medical profession and that of the correctional institution where the medical service is located. In the prison setting, where freedom of choice for both patient and physician is limited, special attention must be given to the personal relationships between patient and doctor to ensure continuity of service, and to foster the development of the best possible patient-doctor relations. Medical services for prisoners must be ever on the alert to recognize and deal constructively with those impediments to patient-physician relationships which may occur in the institutional organization.

The adequacy of the health and medical services is determined by both qualitative and quantitative standards. The quality of the services is determined by the degree to which they reflect the highest standards of medical knowledge and practice. The quantitative aspects are determined by comprehensiveness and balance. Both of these components are essential to any modern correctional medical care program, and are built into the following standards.

Essential Elements of Health and Medical Services

1. Administration

It is incumbent upon the correctional system to provide for a sound medical administrative organization to carry out the duties and responsibilities of the medical care program. Inherent in such a structure is the provision for adequate financial support.

2. Staffing

The full range of modern scientific care can only be carried out by adequate and qualified medical, dental, nursing, laboratory, and other support personnel.

3. Health and Medical Services

The institutional health and medical services must encompass the best knowledge of modern medical science with emphasis upon personal attention and coordination of medical and social treatment effectively organized for continuity and consistency of care.

4. Facilities

The application of all relevant medical services to illness, injury, and defect as well as preventive care for the apparently healthy is enhanced by medical facilities and equipment which meet high technical standards.

Discussion of Objectives and Standards

1. Administration

The administrative structure of a medical care program should be designed to promote democratic control of policy, economy, and efficiency of operation, and quality of medical services. To meet these requirements, the administrative structure of the program must be in harmony with the laws and rules of the medical and related health sciences as well as those of the prison system which it serves. To achieve quality medical care any incompatibility between medical and prison rules must be resolved in the former's favor. Anything less than strict compliance with the laws and rules of the medical profession and its related disciplines will inevitably compromise the quality of the medical care.

A. Agency Structure

The medical division of a correctional system should be directed by a suitably qualified physician assigned as medical director, responsible to the director of the correctional system. The office of the medical director should have sufficient full-time professional and administrative support as is required for the optimal operation of his department. The medical director will play a dual role; first, as staff advisor to the director of corrections, and second, as the senior medical officer in charge of the medical services. The medical director's responsibilities in the latter role include the recruitment, selection, development, and training of all medical personnel, establishment of goals and standards for all correctional institution medical programs, budget development, fiscal control, regular inspections of institution medical facilities and programs, and coordination of research activities.

B. Institutional Structure

The institutional medical services should have a chief medical officer responsible for the administration of the local medical service reporting to the superintendent of his institution and to the medical director of the system. The essential components of good medical administration are: assignment and supervision of personnel; delineation of duties; development of training programs and programs for employee welfare and safety; maintenance of standards of patient care, medical records, physical equipment and plant, development of research and continuing inspection of all aspects of the medical services. Both the medical director and his several chief medical officers must continue to give attention to these elements to insure effective operation of the medical service.

C. Policy and Procedural Manuals

The publication and periodic revision of administrative procedure manuals should help all particpating personnel to understand and attain the desired standards of performance. These manuals should contain both administrative policies and procedures as well as indicated professional routines as established by professional authorities and advisors. To achieve necessary flexibility, provision should be made for the implementation of the administrative procedures into local rules whenever deemed necessary by the chief medical officer in charge of an institution program.

D. Evaluation and Reports

The maintenance of high quality care requires constant self-evaluation against objective criteria established by program administrators. A system should be established for the submission of regular periodic reports covering such aspects of the program as personnel, services rendered, status of equipment and plant, and fiscal management. Finally, the administration should provide for regular audits to check on the standards of service as well as its efficiency.

2. Staffing

The staffing pattern of a given correctional institution should be determined by the health needs of the inmate population and the nature of the health services which are to be provided to personnel. Efficient usage of medical personnel requires that the staff be geared to the population level and commensurate with its needs. In most instances an institutional population's needs will be adequately served if it has immediate recourse to physicians trained in internal medicine, surgery, and psychiartry with access to consultants in other medical specialties such as urology, radiology, opthalmology, ear, nose and throat, and pathology as the need arises. Institution medical staffs should also include dentists and psychologists in sufficient numbers to meet the needs of the inmate population served. Paramedical personnel including nurses, technicians, aides, orderlies, and clerical staff must be provided in sufficient numbers to adequately support the assigned professional personnel. The categories of technicians required in medical programs include laboratory, X-ray, physiotherapy, dental chairside and laboratory, surgical, pharmacy, and electrocardiography. In addition to giving support to the professional staff, paramedical personnel will supervise and train inmates who are assigned to assist with the medical care program.

A. Basic Qualifications

The participation of general practitioners, specialists, and other personnel should be determined by objective qualifications. Physician participation should be restricted to those with degrees of Doctor of Medicine and licenses to practice medicine. Dentists, nurses, and auxiliary personnel should be required to meet appropriate educational and licensure requirements. Standards for medical specialists should be established on the basis of specialty board certification, demonstrated ability, evaluation of previous performance, and standing in the medical community. To insure the best possible care, professional services must be supervised by professional persons.

B. Staff Allocation

The basic medical staff for a penal institution of approximately 500 inmates should include the following: one full-time chief medical officer, one full-time psychiatrist, serving as assistant medical officer, one full-time dental officer, one full-time psychologist, five full-time medical technicians representative of the technical specialties described above and a suitable complement of consultants in the various medical and surgical specialties.

For every additional 500 to 1,000 inmates at least one additional medical officer and medical technician should be added. An additional dental officer is required for each 1,000 additional inmates. In large institutions of over 1,500 inmates, with hospitals having 40 or more beds, consideration should be given to the inclusion of trained registered nurses to insure that the highest nursing standards are maintained with adequate supervision of the operating room as well as the intensive treatment areas. Experience has shown that female nurses can function effectively in the performance of these duties. In smaller institutions, adequate nursing services can be provided by suitably trained medical technicians. However, hospitals depending upon this type of nursing service should have continuous training programs including suitable refresher courses to insure that the nursing skills of the technicians are maintained at an acceptable level.

In addition to the regular full-time hospital employees, sutiably trained inmates should be employed to augment essential paramedical services. These are inmates with adequate intelligence, educational background, and motivation who have been trained as practical nurses, laboratory and X-ray technicians, dental technicians, and physical therapy and operating room aides under the close supervision of medical and correctional personnel. Such training provides prisoners with skills which will facilitate their future adjustment in the community and at the same time, it permits patient care to be extended economically.

C. Dental Program

The principles set down above are all applicable to the establishment of high quality dental care programs. The preventive and protective aspects of dental care should be emphasized along with the provision of essential treatment. Extension of dental services through use of trained auxiliary personnel should be accomplished in correctional institutions as it is in the community at large. As in the medical technical specialties, advantage should be taken of the opportunities which exist for inmate training.

D. Coordination of Services

In the organization of the medical staff, special attention should be given to the coordination of services. The result should be a unified functional relationship between the various categories which make up the medical staff and the subspecialties as provided by the consultant staff. Special attention should be given to the integration of the psychiatric and psychological services into the general medical service to insure that the whole medical staff achieves the best possible understanding of the importance of psychological factors in the management of their patients. The inclusion of psychiatry and psychology into the general medical program can bring about the most effective development of psychiatry within the institution, through the widest possible dissemination and application of sound principles of mental hygiene.

E. Training and Development

Newly assigned medical personnel should be provided with appropriate orientation programs to familiarize them with the prison setting and all aspects of the medical care program in which they are assigned. A high standard of medical practice requires provisions for attendance at professional meetings and postgraduate education courses. Training programs should be implemented for medical technicians and other paramedical workers including inmates. Medical staff should have adequate provision for use of appropriate consultants whenever indicated. Medical personnel should be encouraged to participate in related medical activities in neighboring communities. Reciprocating arrangements with nearby universities in the areas of teaching, training, and research should be developed whenever possible. Finally, the staff should be provided with an adequate reference library, including current texts and journals.

3. Health and Medical Services

Preventive health services at each institution should begin with a physical examination of each newly received inmate, including such laboratory and X-ray studies as may be indicated. Those inmates who are found to be ill upon admission are hospitalized for treatment. As a part of the preventive health program, all new arrivals should receive indicated immunizations and vaccinations. Psychiatric and psychological studies are made whenever indicated. Experience has shown that from 15 to 20 percent of the prisoner population is found to have a diagnosable emotional or mental disorder including neuroses, personality and behavioral disorders, and various types of prepsychotic and psychotic conditions. Suitable screening programs should be developed to insure that all prisoners in need of psychiatric attention are recognized and given indicated treatment. Provision must also be made for the care of those inmates with chronic illness such as the cardiacs, tuberculous and diabetic, and those inmates with chronic mental illness including sexual deviation.

Every prisoner who has a remediable physical condition should be offered suitable medical treatment or surgical correction, to the end that he will be restored to the fullest measure of health prior to his release from the institution. Disfiguring and disabling defects which might interfere with future employment should receive the highest priority in the correctional surgical program. Complete dental care including necessary prosthetic appliances should aslo be provided. Care should also be provided for illness occurring during confinement as well as accidental injuries.

In the preventive health area the medical service should provide inspection and advice on matters relating to institution sanitation including food handling and preparation, milk and water supply, and on industrial health hazards. The medical service has a vital role to play in developing institution mental hygiene programs to prevent the occurrence of disabling mental illness. Preventive services should also include programs for the control of tuberculosis and venereal disease.

At least 10 percent of the institution's population may be expected to visit the outpatient department of the hospital daily either on formal sick line or on special call for examination or treatment. The chief medical officer should exercise close supervision of the outpatient department to insure efficient operation with the provision of a high level of care, responsive to the needs of the inmate population. The outpatient department functions as the center of the health and medical services. The proper conduct of the sick line requires continuing emphasis upon quality care, maintenance of professional decorum, and exploitation of opportunities for health education. The effectiveness of the medical care program is ultimately determined by the responsiveness of the medical staff to the complaint problem which the inmate presents when he visits the outpatient department.

4. Facilities

Effective action to conserve health requries attention to all conditions effecting the health of the individual including such non-medical factors as adequate housing, nutrition, education, and recreation. Medical care must be geared not only to the treatment of disease but also to preventing its occurrence or progress. For those already disabled, all possible use should be made of rehabilitation services so that these individuals may be restored to productive living, free, in so far as possible, of the need for assistance from other members of their families, and able to live as happy and useful lives as possible within the limits of their disabilities. Thus, it is apparent that most measures for the promotion of health must be broadly social or educational in character in order to achieve rehabilitation of the patient in a social as well as a medical sense.

The physical facilities for the medical program should be efficiently arranged to facilitate traffic flow between the various components. Special attention should be given to the design of the outpatient department to facilitate the handling of the daily sick call. The outpatient unit should have an adequate waiting area, consultation rooms, and a treatment area located in reasonable proximity to the clinical laboratory, X-ray, pharmacy, physiotherapy, and the medical record library. The inpatient area of the hospital should provide varied types of accommodations ranging from single rooms to wards in sufficient numbers to handle the anticipated patient load. Inpatient units should include areas for the isolation of patients with contagious disease and appropriate special housing for various types of psychiatric patients who may require security devices for their own safety and well-being. Competent hospital consultant personnel should be employed in the design of hospital units in correctional institutions. Reference should be made to applicable standards and specifications for hospital construction whenever new units or modernization are contemplated.

APPENDIX C

Health Services

Appendix C is excerpted from Chapter 20, pages 178—189, of Manual on Jail Administration *(Washington, D.C.: National Sheriffs' Association, 1970). While the standards of Appendices B and C could, admittedly, be further improved and updated, they do present yardsticks against which prison medical departments can measure themselves.*

Health Services in this chapter encompasses the areas of mental as well as physical health, prevention of disease, dental care, diagnostic examinations, the furnishing of prosthetics, and health education.

For some prisoners, arrest and imprisonment are a blessing in disguise as many have long-neglected ailments which are detected by the jail physician and treated either in the jail or the local hospital. If not so detected, the consequences could have been incapacitating or fatal.

Because of the close proximity of large groups of prisoners in confinement within a small area, which is usually poorly ventilated, it is to be expected that contagious diseases would spread rapidly and affect other prisoners, officers and members of their families, and people in the community with whom they come in contact. It is an important responsibility of the jail to provide the services to diagnose and treat diseases.

The lack of medical attention coupled with improper medical treatment is the most frequent complaint from prisoners. Unfortunately, to a large degree these accusations are justified. Even in jails furnishing excellent medical attention, such complaints are numerous. There are psychological reasons for the prisoner's over-concentration on his body and desire for care and attention, particularly in jails furnishing little or no outlet for physical and mental energies.

The maintenance and improvement of prisoners' health is of vital importance for their adjustment in the jail and for re-entry into the community. It has a direct bearing on the health of residents of the community and is of paramount importance in the efforts of the staff to resocialize the prisoner so that he may be an asset rather than a liability to society.

Standards

1. *Examination of New Prisoners.* Every newly received prisoner should undergo a physical examination before his assignment to a housing area.

2. *A Doctor Always Accessible.* The services of a physician should be available at all times.

3. *Sick Call.* Sick call should be held daily.

4. *Staff.* The health services staff should be adequate for the number of prisoners in the jail.

5. *Community Health Facilities.* Maximum use should be made of community health facilities.

6. *Distribution of Medication.* The distribution of medications to prisoners should be carefully supervised.

7. *Prosthetic Devices.* Necessary prosthetic devices should be furnished to needy prisoners.

8. *Examining Room.* The medical examining room should be adequately equipped.

9. *Infirmary.* An infirmary should be set aside for the housing of prisoners receiving medical treatment within the jail.

10. *Mental Health.* A mental health staff should be available for the examination and diagnosis of every prisoner, and treatment of prisoners who are not sufficiently disturbed to be committed as psychotic.

11. *Sanitation.* A system should be established for keeping the jail in good sanitary condition.

12. *Bathing, Washing, Drinking, and Toilet Equipment.* Adequate bathing, washing, drinking, and toilet equipment should be furnished to the jail population.

13. *Haircutting and Shaving.* Haircutting and shaving facilities should be available.

14. *Medical Records.* Medical records should be kept current for all prisoners.

15. *Rehabilitation.* Medical treatment should aid in the rehabilitation of prisoners.

Discussion of Standards

1. *Examination of Prisoners.*

A prompt and thorough examination of each prisoner is a vital part of the receiving procedure.

    a. It establishes a physical and mental profile of the prisoner.

b. It resolves any questions about whether a prisoner was injured, stricken by illness, or mentally ill, prior to or after entering the jail.

c. A properly kept medical record, initiated at admission, can provide much information that will later prove useful.

d. It detects prisoners in need of immediate or emergency treatment.

e. Proper treatment for certain types of inmates, *e.g.*, drug addicts, diabetics, epileptics, alcholics, infirm prisoners, etc., can be thereby determined.

f. Contraband hidden in body orifices, in prosthetics or under surgical dressings, may be detected by the examining physician.

g. It provides a description of the inmate's scars, tattoos, and other physical features for the identification and medical records.

Newly received prisoners should be kept in a "holding" cell until examination. The examination should be conducted, however, at the earliest practicable moment.

2. *Physician Always Accessible.*

Depending on the number of prisoners, the following alternatives should be considered:

a. A contract can be made with a local physician to be on call to conduct "sick call" and examine newly received prisoners.

b. A contract can be made with a local physician for full-time coverage on certain days.

c. A full-time resident physician can be employed. He may be a medical intern or a student who will work in exchange for room and board.

d. A full-time staff of physicians can be employed and scheduled. One or more would then cover each eight-hour tour of duty.

e. Arrangements can be made with a local hospital for medical services.

3. *Sick Call.*

A definite time should be set daily. This may be:

a. prior to the start of the day's activities, or

b. during recreation periods. (This may lessen malingering.)

Methods of conducting sick call vary. The officer on post should list the names of inmates reporting sick. The physician's examination may be conducted in:

a. the examining room where the inmate has been brought for this purpose;

b. the cell block, with the physician visiting those inmates listed for sick call;

c. the cell block, with the examining room used for selected patients at the discretion of the physician.

An officer should be present:

a. to maintain order.

b. to prevent theft of medication.

c. to prevent arguments with the physician.

All complaints of illness or injury should be noted on the prisoner's medical record together with treatment prescribed.

4. *Staff.*

The size and type of staff depends on the number of prisoners to be served.

a. It may consist of medical doctor or doctors, nurses, technicians, pharmacist(s), medical clerks, psychiatrists, psychologists, psychiatric social worker(s), dentist, optometrist, and consultants.

b. It may be augmented by prisoners who can be trained to function as medical technicians and orderlies.

It has been recommended that an institution of five hundred prisoners should have, on a full-time basis, a minimum of:

a. a chief medical doctor,

b. a technician,

c. a psychiatrist,

d. a psychologist, and

e. a dentist.

An institution of three hundred prisoners should have, on a full-time basis, one physician. An institution of fifty prisoners should have, as an absolute minimum, one full-time nurse.

If the attendance of a full-time nurse or medical technician cannot be obtained, smaller institutions should resort to the alternatives mentioned in the discussion of standard 2. a. through 2. e., above.

The number of physicians and other medical personnel will not only depend on the number of prisoners, but on the desire of the community to provide health care equivalent to that accorded citizens in the free community.

Duties of the medical doctor include:

a. diagnosis,

b. treatment of ailments,

c. prescriptions of medications and special diets,

d. examination of employees when necessary, as in the event of injury or emergency illness or to detect suspected intoxication.

    e. arrangements for hospitalization,

    f. liaison with community facilities,

    g. sanitary inspections,

    h. supervision of the infirmary,

    i. supervision of special treatment programs, as for drug addicts,

    j. approval of restricted diets for punishment,

    k. visitations to solitary confinement prisoners at least twice a day.

Duties of nurses include:

    a. functions related to the care and treatment of prisoners in accordance with the doctor's orders, *e.g.*,

        (1) administration of medications.

        (2) screening cases for the doctor to see.

        (3) supervision of the infirmary.

Duties of technicians include:

    a. operation of equipment for diagnosis and treatment.

    b. laboratory analyses.

    c. those duties of the nurse as the medical doctor may assign, under the supervision of the physician.

Duties of the medical clerk include:

    a. keeping medical records.

    b. typing reports and correspondence.

Duties of the pharmacist include:

    a. ordering stock and safeguarding medications and medical supplies.

    b. filling prescriptions as directed by the doctor.

    c. keeping careful records of inventory, particularly of narcotics, barbiturates, amphetamines, and other dangerous drugs.

Duties of the dentist include:

    a. making dental examinations,

    b. providing emergency treatment,

    c. providing dental treatment when situations permit including the obtaining of dentures,

    d. maintaining dental records.

Duties of the optometrist include:

    a. determination of the need for eyeglasses,

    b. determinations of eyeglass prescriptions,

    c. furnishing of eyeglasses,

    d. referring prisoners with eye diseases to the jail's medical doctor.

Functions of consultants are many. Highly trained specialists may be recruited to provide their services, free of charge, for periodic visits to the jail and to give diagnostic opinions and treatment.

5. *Community Health Facilities.*

A community hospital may be utilized:

a. for cases which cannot be treated adequately in the jail, *e.g.*, surgery and serious ailments.

b. to include a prisoners' jail ward, in which case:

(1) Security features, such as locks, gates, and bars should be installed.

(2) Jail officers should be assigned.

c. for temporary holding of prisoners receiving clinical treatment.

d. for assignment of residents, interns, and medical students to medical functions in the jail.

The Department of Health:

a. sets standards for health treatment,

b. inspects the jail for sanitation and health hazards,

c. provides immunization and treatments, when necessary,

d. provides a portable X-ray machine for tuberculosis diagnosis,

e. investigates epidemics, food poisoning, etc.

f. provides health education.

Mental Health Facilities can provide:

a. mental health staff members for the jail.

b. hospitalization of psychotic prisoners.

c. in-patient and out-patient treatment for discharged prisoners.

d. mental health education.

e. diagnostic examinations for reports and commitments.

The continuity of treatment for discharged prisoners in need of physical or mental treatment, *i.e.*, from the jail to community facilities, should be arranged for by the jail medical staff.

6. *Distribution of Medication.*

All medications should be:

a. administered always under the supervision of a nurse or trusted employee.

b. given in accordance with the doctor's written instructions.

c. dispensed only one dose at a time.

d. swallowed by prisoner, if taken orally. (An accumulation of pills may be bartered or used for a "heavy jolt" or suicide.) Hoarding of medications must be prevented.

7. *Prosthetic Devices.*

A prosthetic device is an artificial part added to the human body to replace one that is lacking such as a leg, an eye, or a tooth. Such a device should be:

a. furnished when necessary for normal function or health while in jail.

b. furnished as an aid to rehabilitation.

c. paid for by the prisoner or from profits from commissary sales. (The Veterans Administration, Medicare, and other sources may pay for prisoners who are qualified to receive benefits from these organizations).

8. *Examining Room.*

An examining room must be equipped with at least the following basic necessities:

a. minimum furniture: desk, chair, examining table, cabinet for supplies,

b. adequate lighting fixtures,

c. minimum equipment: washbasin, scale, electrocardiagraph machine, and drinking fountain,

d. supplies:

(1) Appropriate medications for immediate treatment.

(2) An emergency kit containing hypodermic syringes and needles, tourniquets, hemostats, tongue depressors, and resuscitators.

(3) Instruments, dressings, and material for minor surgery.

(4) A supply of forms for entering medical findings and dispositions.

The need for security precautions in the examining room cannot be overemphasized.

9. *Infirmary.*

An infirmary may be used to house:

a. prisoners with such minor ailments as a respiratory disease.

b. prisoners with minor ailments who need more intensive medical care for short periods of time.

c. prisoners who are crippled, aged, and infirm. They may be housed in a special area in the infirmary away from those with contagious diseases.

10. *Mental Health.*

Mental health care is vitally important. Many prisoners are emotionally disturbed, some are pre-psychotic, and others may be psychotic but in a temporary state of remission. Even these ostensibly "normal" prisoners may benefit from some form of treatment. To provide this treatment, the services of a professional social worker, psychologist, or psychiatrist, either individually or as a mental health team, are necessary. They should coordinate their efforts with the medical staff.

The duties of the psychiatrist include:

a. diagnosis of mental illness.

b. prescription of medication or other treatment for mental illness.

c. to provide psychotherapy, individual and/or group.

d. certification of mentally ill prisoners.

e. submission of reports to authorized agencies.

f. acting as chief of the mental health team.

The duties of the psychologist include:

a. administration and evaluation of psychological tests, *e.g.*, intelligence tests, personality, and aptitude tests.

b. performance of some duties of the psychiatrist, if qualified, except for prescription of medications.

The duties of the social worker include:

a. some duties of the psychologist, if qualified to do so.

b. relating test results and psychiatric diagnosis to the patient's social situation. The prisoner's family situation, community adjustment, employment and general adjustment are all relevant to a mental illness.

11. *Sanitation.*

Sanitation practices are necessary for preventing disease. All of the following recommendations should be considered in planning for sanitation in the jail.

a. Establish a schedule for cleaning every area in the entire jail.

b. Provide proper and sufficient cleaning supplies. (Do not use disinfectants.)

c. Establish a system whereby daily sanitation inspections will be conducted to ascertain cleanliness.

d. Provide for medical examination of food handlers, barbers, and medical orderlies at frequent intervals.

e. Prohibit the accumulation of any materials in the housing areas.

f. Provide for proper refrigeration and storage of food.

g. Provide adequate ventilation.

h. Provide freshly laundered linen to be issued at least once each week.

12. *Bathing, Washing, Drinking, and Toilet Equipment.*

Personal cleanliness is no less important than institutional cleanliness. For this reason, the following fixtures should be provided:

a. Showers. The number of shower stalls should be appropriate for the number of prisoners, *e.g.,* three shower stalls for twenty individual cells or a twenty-five bed dormitory.

(1) Individual showers should be made available in the housing area. Each prisoner should shower at least twice weekly.

(2) Group showers must be scheduled for housing areas or work groups.

(3) Food handlers should shower at least once daily, perhaps more often.

(4) Showers should be prescribed daily for prisoners on certain work details.

b. Washbowls (lavatories): There should be:

(1) One washbowl in each single cell.

(2) One washbowl for each eight prisoners in a multiple cell or dormitory.

c. Drinking fountains. These should be provided in cells, dormitories, recreation areas, and waiting rooms. They may be:

(1) a sink tap, or preferably

(2) a sink spout.

d. Toilets. Adequate facilities must be provided. For sanitary and security reasons, each cell should have at least one toilet. Multi-occupied rooms should have at least one toilet for each eight inmates.

13. *Haircutting and Shaving.*

Excessive hair growth must be avoided for sanitary reasons. Provisions must therefore be made for haircutting and shaving of prisoners.

a. Haircutting. The services of a barber or barbers must be procured. Each person used as a barber should undergo a thorough medical examination.

Barber services may be arranged by:

(1) establishing a barber school in the jail with a qualified civilian barber to instruct the inmates, or

(2) by using barber students from the community.

Prisoners' hair should be reasonably short. Shaving of the head should be done only by order of the medical doctor, for medical reasons. When hair on an unconvicted prisoner is considered unsanitary, he may be isolated until he consents to having it cut to an acceptable length.

b. Shaving. Each prisoner may normally be expected to shave himself. Instruments must be furnished to him in most cases.

(1) locked safety razors should be issued.

(2) electric razors may be permitted if they are the prisoner's personal property.

(3) Individual razors may be allowed for certain prisoners, *e.g.*, work release and minimum security inmates.

Prisoners should not have unsightly beards.

(1) Beards may be removed for purposes of sanitation and identification.

(2) Prisoners should be cleanly shaven before court appearances and visits.

14. *Medical Records.*

Medical records are necessary for:

a. providing a case history for reference.

b. providing information necessary for answering complaints relative to injuries and treatment.

c. forwarding to the receiving institution when the prisoner is transferred.

d. use in institutional classification.

e. use by the courts.

15. *Rehabilitation.*

Rehabilitation has many facets. Its benefits and services include:

a. rendering the prisoner fit to participate in jail treatment programs.

b. rendering the prisoner better able to earn a living upon his release.

c. providing corrective surgery.

d. providing cosmetic surgery when deemed necessary.

e. providing for continuity of treatment from the jail to the community.

Glossary

To the uninitiated, a casual conversation among a group of inmates might be difficult to follow because of the level of idiom usage.

This specialized language seems to vary from facility to facility; perhaps someday an enterprising scholar will analyze these terms and compile the first truly comprehensive "Inmates' Dictionary."

Until that time, Appendix D is presented to give the reader a flavor of the language. This appendix is an adaptation of a glossary that was prepared for volunteers by the Rehabilitation Department of the Orleans Parish Prison in New Orleans, Louisiana.

Inmate—The more acceptable term for the prisoner.

Tier—A section of the prison; one wing on one floor; name for cellblock or inmate location.

Hospital—A tier location for inmates, it also houses the dentist's office; referred to often by some inmates as the 'pital.

Swing—To swing a man is to transfer him from his prison job to a lock-down tier, which is usually done as a disciplinary measure.

The Hole—Maximum security cells.

Roll-In—Entering the prison as an inmate.

Roll-Out—To be released from prison.

Shakedown—An inspection or search of a tier or an inmate designed to discover contraband, such as weapons or narcotics.

Knock-Down—Banging on the bars of the tier, in unison, by inmates to attract attention.

Fall-Partner—One of two or more men charged at the same time for the same offense.

Cop a Plea, or Cop Out—To plead guilty to a charge at time of arraignment in order to eliminate the long wait for trial.

Rap-Sheet—The sheet or sheets outlining a man's police record.

Hold—A detainer placed against an inmate in order to prevent his release when he is wanted on another charge than the one he is serving sentence for.

Yank, Yank Gang—A work crew which regularly cleans the corridors and offices of the prison. They are likely to be called (yanked) from their tiers for odd jobs at odd hours.

Kite—A written communication between inmates, usually on another tier. These are forbidden.

Bust—To be arrested.

Hallboy—An inmate assigned as an orderly on a tier. He also keeps order on the tier he is assigned.

Flat Time—The length of time the judge has determined. Credit for time served is given for the days spent in prison waiting for trial. They are subtracted from the total flat time sentence. Good time can be given only for the days after sentencing.

Good Time—Good time can be earned. The sheriff and warden may award good time, up to one-half of the sentence, in return for cooperation. All of the following is considered when giving good time:

    1. Willingness to work at assigned prison job.
    2. Prompt reporting when called by deputies or runners.
    3. Good behavior.
    4. Participation in all assigned rehabilitation programs and activities. These activities include:

        a. Interviews
        b. Testing
        c. Counseling
        d. School
        e. Discussion groups
        f. Pre-release
        g. Special projects

DATE DUE

DEC 16 78			
NOV 1 78			
APR 2 1981			
APR 9 1981			
MAY 2 0 1981			
NOV 2 0 1986			
JUN 8 1989			